KT-438-717

Non-Verbal Learning Disabilities
Characteristics, Diagnosis and Treatment within an Educational Setting

Marieke Molenaar-Klumper

NORWICH CITY COLLEGE LIBRARY

Stock No.   193461

Class   618.9285889 mol

Cat.   Proc.   IWL

Jessica Kingsley Publishers
London and Philadelphia

All rights reserved. No part of this publication may be reproduced in any material form (including photocopying or storing it in any medium by electronic means and whether or not transiently or incidentally to some other use of this publication) without the written permission of the copyright owner except in accordance with the provisions of the Copyright, Designs and Patents Act 1988 or under the terms of a licence issued by the Copyright Licensing Agency Ltd, 90 Tottenham Court Road, London, England W1P 9HE. Applications for the copyright owner's written permission to reproduce any part of this publication should be addressed to the publisher.

Warning: The doing of an unauthorised act in relation to a copyright work may result in both a civil claim for damages and criminal prosecution.

The right of Marieke Molenaar-Klumper to be identified as author of this work has been asserted by her in accordance with the Copyright, Designs and Patents Act 1988.

First Published in Dutch in 2001 under the title of *NLD - Signaleren, diagnosticeren en behandelen in de onderwijssetting* by Swets & Zeitlinger Publishers, Lisse.

First published in the United Kingdom in 2002
by Jessica Kingsley Publishers Ltd
116 Pentonville Road
London N1 9JB, England
and
325 Chestnut Street
Philadelphia, PA 19106, USA
www.jkp..com

Copyright © Jessica Kingsley Publishers 2002

Library of Congress Cataloging in Publication Data
A CIP catalog record for this book is available from the Library of Congress

British Library Cataloguing in Publication Data
A CIP catalogue record for this book is available from the British Library

ISBN 1 84310 066 5

Printed and Bound in Great Britain by
Athenaeum Press, Gateshead, Tyne and Wear

Contents

Acknowledgements

This book was written during the time I spent at De Brug, the institute in Leiden (September 1998 – June 1999). The institute, which is like a typical school, with its systematic observation, treatment and development of new insights to support its practice, formed the basis for this book. The first version was published in 1999 as a brochure and was intended as information for people directly involved in the education of children with NLD. Furthermore, the brochure was distributed to teachers throughout the Leiden District. The tremendous amount of positive reactions that the brochure generated led to the development of this book. Without the support of my colleagues at De Brug none of this would have been possible. Enthusiastic reactions, critical questions, constructive remarks and people keeping their eyes open for new articles on NLD helped the book become what it is today.

I would like to thank the following people personally: Koen van Zoest (treatment coordinator/pedagogue), Anne-Lies Besemer (treatment coordinator and psychotherapist), Suzanne Kluivers (teacher), Elske Purmer (teacher) Anneke Sumer (language teacher), Marjolein Tuijthoff (remedial teacher) and Kees Beintema (PI headmaster). They, amongst other things, took part in the resonance group and gave valuable input and comments in relation to their respective academic and professional backgrounds. I would also like to thank Anneke Boelens, "Joyce's" teacher at the time, who let me come into the classroom at will and let me observe her whenever I saw fit. Her willingness to adjust her approach in the classroom so as not to disrupt my individual approach, and the informal chats I had with her proved to be very useful. I would like to thank Mieke Bernard (remedial teacher) who took Joyce's maths tutoring over from me; thank you for letting me look over your shoulder. I thank also Joyce's parents for putting their trust in me. All my colleagues who attended my seminars and whose insights and comments contributed to my book, I thank you all!

I am grateful to the Pedagogical Institute, as a school and as an institute, and especially to the Directors, for the opportunity they gave me to delve into this interesting subject. Without the input of the school, the brochure would never have become a book. And last but not least, I thank my family and husband who got me through the most difficult of times (apparently they are a common accompaniment to writing a book) with warmth and love.

About the Author

Marieke Molenaar-Klumper has been working as a pedagogue at the Pedagogical Institute in Leiden since 1998. At the De Brug school which is tied to the Institute, she gained experience in the field of treating children with NLD. Her clinical experience was, in many ways, a welcome addition to the information she gathered from already existing literature within the field.

Teaching methods and materials

Capital-letter writing method with De Leessleutel (*Blokschrift*); M. Tuythoff-Pera (1998) Leiden: Pedological Institute – De Brug.

Gradual reading and language skills (*De Leessleutel*); R. Berends e.a. (1997) Den Bosch: Malmberg.

A box full of feelings (*Een doos vol gevoelens*); Kog & J. Moons (1999) Leuven: Centrum Ervaringsgericht Onderwijs (Centre for Experience-orientated education).

Programme for the development of visual perception (*Frostig*); M. Frostig, L. Richardson and B. Mandell (1974) Lisse: Swets & Zeitlinger.

Letterfun, teaching method for gradual reading and spelling (*Letterpret*); J. Lips (1992) Leiden: Institute.

My own handwriting, computer programme (*Mijn eigen handschrift*); M. Lindeman (1996) Houten: Educative Partners Nederland BV.

Modular Construction (*Modulair Construction I en II*); Work group Rolf Didactic, Ochten: Rolf Onderwijs BV.

M.J.Elzer and K.Freriks (1991) PATHS-Curriculum M.T (*PAD-leerplan*); Greenberg, C.A.Kusche, R. Calderon and R. Gustafson (1987) Utrecht: FODOK & SvO.

General guide (*PILAAR*); E. Tijhuis (1996) Leiden: The Institute.

Mathematical Support (*Speciaal Rekenhulpprogramma*); J.E.H. van Luit and R. van der Krol (1989). Doetinchem: Graviant.

The Little Maths-man, dealing with problems with addition and subtraction (*Het Rekenmannetje*); J.W.M van Erp (1989) Groningen: Wolters Noordhoff.

Maths for children with learning difficulties (*Remelka*); G. Eijkhout-van Rooij, L. Erich, S. Huitema, J. Loos, J. Rijs & T. Schippers. **Den Bosch**: Malmberg.

List of abbreviations

ADHD: Attention Deficit Hyperactivity Disorder

AS: Asperger Syndrome

ASD: Autistic Spectrum Disorder

CBCL: Child Behavior Checklist

Cito: Central Institute for Test Development

DSM-IV: Developmental Statistical Manual of Mental Disorders

HCP: Home Contingency Plan

ICD-9: International Classification of Diseases

MRT: Motor Remedial Teaching

NLD: Non-verbal Learning Difficulties

NLD-Scale: Scale of Non-verbal Learning Difficulties

PAD: Programma Alternatieve Denkstrategieen (Programme of Alternative Thinking Strategies)

PDD-NOS: Pervasive Developmental Disorder – Not Otherwise Specified

PI: Pedagogical Institute

PILAAR: Pedologisch Instituut Leiden Aanvankelijk Rekenen (Pedagogical Institute for Gradual Mathematics, Leiden)

PIQ: Performance Intelligence Quotient

RAKIT: Revisie van de Amsterdamse Kinder Intelligentietes (Revision of the Amsterdam Children's Intelligence Test)

REC: Regionaal Expertise Centrum (Regional Centre of Expertise)

TRF: Teacher Report Form

TvK: Taaltest voor Kinderen (Language Test for Children)

VIQ: Verbal Intelligentie Quotient (Verbal Intelligence Quotient)

VMI: Developmental test of Visual Motor Integration (Beery)

WISC-RN: Wechsler Intelligence Scale for Children – Revised

WS: Williams Syndrome

Introduction

He'll talk until you drop. He knows something about everything. He knows all these difficult words. Sometimes you feel as if you're talking to a teenager when in reality he's only seven years old. You would think that he's extremely smart, yet he's having trouble in the third grade. When it comes to mathematics, he understands very little: "He doesn't understand numbers," the teacher explains. Writing is also something he's having trouble with. It's as if he can't remember what a letter looks like. Reading came about slowly, and luckily is getting better now. He's pretty clumsy when he has to get dressed or tidy up – he simply doesn't know where to begin. He really dislikes physical education and manual labor (woodwork etc.), maybe because he hasn't really mastered coordination. Even though this is his third year in school, he keeps getting lost in the corridors. He is very curious, though, and asks the teacher a lot of questions. He likes sitting close to her and even during recess he tends to look around for her. He finds it quite difficult to make friends.

This book is an introduction to the subject of NLD, and can be a stepping-stone for further research and discussion. The ultimate objectives of this book are:

- to raise awareness of the symptoms of NLD

- the identification of characterisitcs need to be looked for to bring about a speedy diagnosis of NLD

- to show how to discover the unmistakable signs of NLD in children

- to introduce possible ways of approaching this issue.

The educational setting of De Brug (The Bridge), a school affiliated to the Pedagogical Institute (PI) of Leiden, is used as a starting point. The population of this school is made up of children aged 3–13 who have complex, difficult problems adjusting to scholastic life. From this setting, the book is aimed at anyone who works with children who have serious learning and behavioral problems. Teachers, classroom assistants, counselors/supporters, remedial teachers, psychologists, therapists and social workers are the groups of people the book is aimed at. The insights it provides are not only applicable to special schools; they can also be of use in other educational establishments.

The book opens with an elaborate case description. Then, in Chapter 1 ("What is NLD?") a relatively complete outline is given of the typical developmental characteristics and course of development of a child who has NLD, in the areas of cognitive, psychometric, socio-emotional and special capacities. The child's scholastic development is also discussed. The chapter ends with a definition of NLD. In Chapter 2 ("Characteristics of NLD"), two developmental profiles are described that will help make early recognition easier. Chapter 3 ("Diagnosing NLD") shows which diagnostic instruments can be used if one suspects a child has NLD. In Section 3.2 a preliminary investigation is made into the way the manifestations of NLD are different from those of other psychiatric ailments in children that are described in textbooks. In this same section, critical questions are asked about the existence of NLD. Concrete treatment strategies, applicable both at home and at school and a perspective on the futures of children with NLD feature in Chapter 4 ("Treatment of NLD"). The book ends with a few recommendations in the Epilogue.

Many articles and books have been written about NLD. Even today, experimental research takes place and new discoveries are made. This books gives, in an integrated way, an overview of most of the opinions expressed in both Dutch and English publications. The author hopes that this publication moves people towards specific focal points associated with the characteristics and, as a consequence, the treatment of NLD.

Leiden, October 2000
Marieke Molenaar-Klumper

Case study

The case study of Joyce is based on fact, but it has been adjusted to protect the privacy of those concerned. Therefore Joyce is a pseudonym.

During the scholastic year beginning in September 1998, Joyce was intensively guided by the author, due to her diagnosis of NLD. During this exceptional form of remedial teaching (three hours a week), attention was paid to Joyce's ways of studying and the ways in which she dealt with subject matter in the areas of reading, spelling, writing and mathematics. Furthermore, the author tried to train her visual-spatial capacities. The approach was based, on one hand, on the still limited information available from Dutch literature on NLD, and, on the other hand, on the more general principles of treatment for children with a learning disorder. Traits of NLD discovered during this treatment process are given as examples throughout this book. To understand the examples better, some background information about Joyce follows. It illustrates the difference made to Joyce's developmental progress after her placement at the school in Leiden.

Joyce

Joyce's history

Joyce was born in 1991, and at the age of six she was brought to a special school because of her problematic development in her third year in primary school. From the results of tests, we know that her problems did not originate from her mother's pregnancy. Joyce was a happy baby. Her parents tell us that she had started to crawl, sit, stand and walk at the normal ages that you would expect. After a period of one and half years of baby-talk, Joyce began uttering her first few full words. As a toddler she was very expressive and independent and often ventured out on her own.

When Joyce was three, her parents experienced some difficulties with her; she was much less talkative and became very closed up and shy. She had difficulty focusing on a task at hand and reacted very badly to new situations. Her parents got the impression that she was an under-achiever in school, and that she tried to escape situations in which she was expected to perform. Tidying up and getting changed were difficult chores. She often interrupted people in the middle of a sentence with questions about technical or historical issues, or in some cases just to tell a story. She had an easier time being around adults than children. When she was rejected by others, she continued to ask questions (as a way of attracting attention) and demand attention.

At the age of six, her social life was very hard. Joyce reacted in a very impulsive and egocentric way when she spoke to other children. With adults she was both verbally and physically demanding. She spoke in a pseudo-adult manner and asked a lot of complicated questions.

When it came to understanding things, one noticed a strong and quickly developing vocabulary and a very weak IQ (78 at the age of 6), which made it hard for Joyce to deal with perceptual challenges. Joyce had difficulty with order and insufficient understanding of time and space. She also showed signs of dyspraxia. Her self-sufficiency was far from what it should have been. She had problems making structure in her dealings and was easily distracted. When faced with a situation that was new to her, she found it difficult to focus. Her impulse reduction and sensory regulation were inadequate, which brought the possibility of ADHD to the forefront of her condition. She showed signs verging on socio-emotional and cognitive breakdown, despite intensive remedial teaching. Because of complex developmental problems, with possible cerebral function irregularities, the decision was made in August 1997 to put her in the special Pedagogical Institute school in Leiden (De Brug).

At the PI School in Leiden

Joyce arrived at the school at the age of six and a half. From the start, it was thought she might have NLD, possibly in combination with ADHD. Verbally, Joyce made a big impression. She got into conversations with every adult, talked while doing her work and asked many questions. Because of her use of language, it was possible to overestimate her. Her unrest was expressed mostly by the fact that she lost concentration very easily and talked a lot. Her visual perceptions were quite weak, although she did understand things if they were explained to her verbally. A consultation with the resident child neurologist in the autumn of 1997 showed the likelihood of a non-verbal learning disability (NLD), with her right hemisphere seeming to be specifically problematic. From that moment onwards, the people working with Joyce have had NLD as a basis to work from.

During her placement, a couple of typically NLD-related symptoms came to the forefront of Joyce's behavior. Her intelligence pattern showed a severe disharmonic profile: her verbal potential was more developed than her performance potential. Psychometrically, her undeveloped finger coordination, her weak refinement sensors, her weak body language and the very weak flexing of her muscles showed an overall weakness. Her verbal strength was expressed in a very broad vocabulary, a constant flow of words when spoken to, excellent grammatical speech and a good capability of associating words with one another. Joyce gave herself internal structure by giving her manual dealings verbal guidance. In her schoolwork she was very untidy and she failed to bring structure to her handwriting and to the content of what she was writing about. To teach Joyce something new, a lot of repetition was necessary. Once she had learnt something, after many repetitions, she could do it almost perfectly. A game was designed, in which she talked herself through her actions.

Socially, she had a hard time considering the other party. She often took on a certain role and conflicts occured regularly. At home she also found herself in conflicts with her brothers and sisters. Her parents made a big effort to give Joyce a structured day. They had a difficult time with her uninhibited behavior. At home, she would walk into anyone's room at any time and have a long conversation.

At the end of the intensive remedial teaching, Joyce was eight and a half years old. The two years she spent in Leiden were filled with small steps forward but also some sudden setbacks. Her technical reading is coming about, but with a lot of practice. Her writing has made some good progress, but her visual coordination is not what it should be for a child her age and it sometimes worsens suddenly. Mathematics is Joyce's weakest point. She has a hard time doing sums with numbers ranging from one to ten. This is due to the fact that she still doesn't *understand* numbers. Her visual-spatial ability remains a hurdle, although with more training it could still improve. She is now more capable of digesting information. She is experiencing growth; she makes small steps forward and from time to time a big step backwards.

Examples from Joyce's treatment can be found in Chapters 1 and 4.

CHAPTER 1

What is NLD?

This chapter provides a first impression of the features and background of NLD. Attention is given to its definition (Section 1.1), characteristics (Section 1.2), development in school (Section 1.3), the causes and underlying mechanisms of the syndrome and its frequency (Section 1.4). Finally, an explanatory model of NLD is presented (Section 1.5).

1.1 Definition

NLD is defined as a neuropsychological syndrome and stands for Non-verbal Learning Disabilities. After research into various sub-categories of learning difficulties (Johnson and Myklebust 1967, in Hellemans 1995), Myklebust (1975, in Hellemans 1995, and in Cracco 1993) brought the term "non-verbal learning disabilities" to the forefront for the very first time. Later, NLD was thoroughly studied by Rourke (1989), who in turn defined the syndrome from a developmental neuropsychological approach. NLD is described as a right- hemisphere malfunction or as an information-processing malfunction that is characterized by its close relationship with learning and behavioral difficulties caused by lack of mental coordination. NLD is also referred to as "planlessness" or the non-cooperation of neuro-psychological, scholastic, socio-emotional and adaptive functions (Rourke 1989). Shortages and a general lack in primary, secondary, tertiary and verbal neuropsychological developments take their toll on scholastic performance and socio-emotional functioning (see Section 1.5). Therefore, a specific profile of NLD comes to light. Shortcomings and talents in learning ability on the one hand, and more shortcomings from a socio-emotional and adaptive point of view on the other, are typical manifestations.

In the 1970s there was a realization that there is not just *one* type of learning disability. Since then, a lot of research has been undertaken from a neuropsychological viewpoint that has led to the conclusion that there are several subtypes of learning disabilities, and that each demands a different approach. Rourke's research (1989, 1993a) eventually led to a description of the NLD syndrome. From various studies on children with learning disabilities, Rourke described three subtypes:

- group 1: weak reading, spelling and mathematical skills

- group 2: weak reading and spelling, just below average in mathematics

- group 3: average reading and spelling, very weak in mathematics.

The children in group 1 did not form a homogenous group. With all the children in group 2 there appeared to be a question of left-hemisphere difficulties, and all the childen in group 3 showed clear right-hemisphere difficulties. The profile of group 3 is identical to the NLD profile. What makes this so is the fact that the children in this group have difficulty processing information in the right half of their brain. This concerns what is called the inter-modal tasks (Costa and Goldberg 1981, in Rourke 1989). These are tasks where several different pieces of information need to be combined with one another. An example of one of these tasks is tying one's shoelaces. For the NLD child, processing new understandings, solving problems and learning from past experiences are difficult. However, if the thinking process happens through the left side of the brain, the child shows considerably less difficulty. In this case, inter-modal tasks are involved, for which previously known information is needed. Routine tasks and stereotypical patterns, such as the reciting of repetitively studied timetables, are easy for these children. The information stored in the left side of the brain is more easily accessible as it has a simpler structure. The information in the right side of the brain is stored in a branch-like structure. For an NLD child, this seems to make accessing the information more complex and confusing (Serlier-Van den Bergh, in Langelaan 1999).

1.2 Characteristics

Rourke (1989, in Serlier-van den Bergh *et al.* 1997) comes to the conclusion that a child's basic abilities have three aspects: shortages in psychomotor coordination, in exploring behavior and in perception. Together with these, problems are often found in developmental levels, activity levels, speech/ language, emotions, social behavior and the ability to adapt. Problematic and atypical development of these levels and abilities can be recognized in every child with NLD and hence form the basis of the NLD image. The older the child gets, the clearer these problems become. There is, however, a nuance:

not all characteristics will be as clear and as visible in every child.

1.2.1 Psychomotor coordination

The term "psychomotor coordination" is not only relevant to behavior; it also concerns the guidance and coordination that is developed in the brain. Both basic coordination and finer coordination skills develop very slowly and lag behind in the average NLD child. Although it seems to be a case of bilateral lack of coordination, the left-hand side of the child's body is often less developed. Left-handedness is very rare among NLD children. One sign of NLD that can be seen at a very young age is that the child tries to avoid crossing the two sides of his/her body, for example, not crossing their legs or arms. Also, the child may experience problems in maintaining balance – for example, after a NLD toddler is picked up and put down again, s/he might not regain the correct position automatically (Thompson 1997b).

The NLD child has great difficulty with movement patterns where coordination is required (e.g. tying shoelaces, eating, getting dressed, climbing). Hence a toddler often does not want to eat with a fork or spoon. The toddler will move very technically and in a wooden manner, s/he may have a fear of heights or may have difficulty with coordination when it comes to writing. In this case the child's grip on the pen or pencil will be very strenuous and tense and a lot of pressure will be applied onto the paper to try to exert control.

The combination of several actions is very problematic. NLD children have difficulty maintaining good posture due to their lack of coordination. As soon as the child has to eat or read s/he forgets about posture and slumps almost immediately.

Concentrating on how to have a good grip on her pen while trying to do something else at the same time (the actual writing) was very difficult for Joyce. As soon as she started to write or read, she slumped over her desk and her fingers took on a bad position.

During her swimming lesson, Joyce found it very difficult to swim forward by moving her legs while at the same time holding a ball ahead of her. In the changing room, Joyce was quite slow. This was because there were so many children in the changing room that she forgot to pay attention to herself.

Only after a lot of repetition can improvements be made. NLD children prefer doing stereotypical movement patterns. The combination of their weaknesses in coordination and inability to assess where something is in time and space also makes NLD children more accident-prone and more likely to be socially rejected.

1.2.2 Exploration

Assuming that the processing of information does not run smoothly when from the right side of the brain, the child will not discover much by looking (visual) or feeling (tactile). NLD children are visually and spatially impaired in their exploration of the world hence they are limited in their knowledge of the world. Even from a young age, NLD children prefer to explore through listening (audio) and through asking many questions (verbal) and hardly ever through looking and moving.

Joyce explored the world through verbal channels, just by sitting on her chair and asking many questions, whereas a "normal" child would be more likely to look at and touch everything. Joyce would ask questions like: Where do you live? Who is in the room next door? What's behind that

curtain? What's that noise in the corridor? Who does that
computer belong to?

When the audio/verbal side of the child with NLD has
developed, s/he is likely to engage less in physical exploration;
exploration through hearing and sight delivers enough
information (Dumont 1994). The world stays simple for the
child if s/he just asks and listens. Names are given to shallow
visual impressions. Other aspects of the world (e.g. how does it
feel, how far is it, why does it change size the closer you get to
it?) barely get explored. Paternotte (1999a, p.20) recounts the
story of Aunt Gertrude's Vase (Rourke 1995). Mother is
visiting Aunt Gertrude with her child. Aunt Gertrude has a
wonderful collection of antiques but, more importantly, she
has a beautiful vase. Normally, a child would go exploring
around the house. There's a ten-to-one chance that the child
will knock over the vase and break it. However, it is unlikely
that the child who breaks the vase will be the one with NLD. It
could be a child that does not research his world and tries to
avoid new situations. The NLD child asks "What's that?" and
he gets as an answer "That's Aunt Gertrude's vase". The child
trains his verbal skills; he has learnt that those things are called
vases and it has something to do with Aunt Gertrude. Other
children would have gone up to the vase and used their eyes,
coordination and visual memory. They learn to estimate and
see distance, and learn to combine seeing and moving. They
touch the vase and thereby train their tactile skills and develop
a tactile memory. They lift the vase and experience gravity.
They drop the vase, hear the porcelain smash on the floor and
spread all throughout the room. They experience their parents'
reaction and realize what is socially permitted and what is not.
For these children, when they hear the word "vase", they have a
collection of audio-visual and tactile information to draw

upon. The NLD child hasn't acquired this, through lack of exploration.

The limited will to explore is expressed by a preference for known dealings and familiar things, as NLD children have difficulty with motor coordination (e.g. climbing) and prefer to digest information through audio-visual media than any other. They can't trust their own movements or spatial considerations. Often one will notice the NLD child staring blankly ahead. This staring can be interpreted as a way of closing him/herself from the multitude of visual stimuli s/he is faced with and does not know how to digest. As a consequence of the limited need to explore and poor coordination, the child shows very little interest in creative lessons at school like art or woodwork.

1.2.3 Perception

NLD children are quite good at noticing details, but have difficulty separating them from the whole of the object that is being perceived. The child might, for example, be able to describe a house in the smallest detail, but not know where the house is. The way NLD children perceive the world is related to development and thinking in a spatial context.

The development of the thinking process is thought to happen very slowly in NLD children. This is because their ability to analyze, organize and synthesize is weak (Smeets and Van de Wiel 1996). Furthermore, they have very few environmental impressions due to their lack of exploration. As a consequence, they have difficulties with forming understandings of places and situations, with logical reasoning and with problem solving. This inability is more noticeable when more formal-operational thinking is required (second half of primary school). Most NLD children have normal intelligence, but there is a substantial difference between their verbal and visual-spatial intelligence, the latter being the weaker. When the child is less gifted, the weaknesses are more apparent. The NLD child learns little from experience. Every even slightly different situation is regarded as a new one. The memory for new complex material and for difficult verbal information is very limited and weak.

> When Joyce went to a class, for example mathematics, and the class was given in a different room than usual, Joyce would forget the usual routine of switching on the light when walking into the room and putting the "do not disturb" sign on the door. She considered this lesson a completely new experience, with no precedent, because it was not in the setting she was used to, even though it was practically identical to a situation that she had already experienced.

In facing new situations, the child relies on verbal memories. S/he is unable to identify what is different about the new situation, and will respond to it in a limited way, based on verbal memory of a somewhat similar situation. She reacts in an inappropriate stereotypical manner.

NLD children are known to have weak visual-spatial capacity. Sometimes it is referred to as a left/right-orientation problem. In their perception, NLD children put an emphasis on details instead of on the situation in its entirety. Their ability to compare different facets (breadth, length, height, color, etc.) of an object in space is underdeveloped.

> In a drawing-by-numbers exercise, Joyce drew a horse. At first, she didn't recognize the image. Only after she had examined the page a while longer and had been given a few hints, did she recognize it as a horse.
>
> Joyce has great difficulty seeing a letter or a number as a full visual whole. To her, letters and numbers are, and will be, loose bits of information that she has difficulty putting

down on paper together as a whole. In her mind, a letter or number does not have one basic shape, therefore, when put down on paper, it can take on many shapes. Only after long repetitious studying will she be capable of writing it down correctly.

Due to poorly developed visual–spatial insight, NLD children have difficulty doing a familiar activity in a new place. They need all their concentration in order to orientate themselves. Small changes to a familiar situation can also completely confuse them.

One day, Joyce noticed that an armrest on one of the chairs she usually sits on had come loose. Joyce immediately reacted to this by declaring that she could not work on that chair anymore. The same happens when she sits on a different chair than she's used to; she needs time to adjust.

The realization of time is also a weakness with NLD children. The concept of time and of time going by during a day or activity are phenomena that are strange. As a consequence of their visual–spatial difficulties, they will rarely play with construction blocks, so they do not have to face problems of calculation. Mathematical exercises are practically impossible for these children to imagine visually.

NLD children can get an enormous fright from loud noises, like the school bell or the shuffling of chairs or desks along a floor somewhere else in the building. They may be hearing sounds in an amplified form, because they are more used to digesting audio information. Their capacity to hear is far better developed than their capacity to see or feel.

1.2.4 Activity level

Typical of the development of NLD children is their fluctuating activity level. Especially with a young NLD child, there is clearly a very short attention span. There is also a question of impulsive behavior – throwing themselves into a situation and then acting as though they are completely detached from that situation. Paternotte (1998) blames this on the child's estimation that there is pressure around him/her; this explains the child's busy hectic behavior. The child then realizes that s/he is surrounded by high expectations and abandons what s/he started and sometimes gets very upset. S/he starts behaving very chaotically and basically loses control. This is why people may get the impression the child has ADHD. An attention problem is not one of the basic characteristics of the NLD profile, and does not present itself in every situation. Although attention to visual and tactile information is limited, the child concentrates well on verbal information and simple repetitive material. Furthermore, as said earlier, there is a question of fluctuating activity levels – the hyperactive, busy and uninhibited behavior exhibited at the age of four or five years old (which has its roots in weak tactile development) normalizes after a while. It could possibly even turn into hypo-active behavior (very calm, passive and pathetic: Dumont 1994; Bachot, Duits and Graauwmans 1996). As a consequence of being rejected by the people around them and failures in diverse areas of their scholastic life, NLD children start to develop a lack of initiative. When they reach adolescence and puberty, they may have a passive, withdrawn behavioral pattern. In some cases, this can turn into depression.

1.2.5 Language/Speech

When NLD children are babies, their language/speech development is very slow. It is often speculated that they could be deaf or mute. When they are toddlers, they start developing speech at a quicker pace. They talk a lot, with a large vocabulary, and know something about almost everything. A parent said of her son: "Once he got started, there was no stopping him. He brought up everything he knew. Sometimes I cringed because he told everyone intimate details of our family life. We thought that was quite childish for a child of seven. Most children at that age have already gained a sense of what is appropriate and what is not." (Paternotte 1999d, pp. 20–21).

NLD children will talk themselves through any situation that may arise.

> While doing a drawing, Joyce talks more than she actually draws. She gives a detailed plan of what she's doing/about to do without putting much down onto paper. The talking goes before the drawing – she first tells of what she'll draw and then starts drawing. While drawing, Joyce puts what she's doing into words: "And now I'll draw a little house, smoke is coming out of the chimney, a few windows…"

Because of the NLD child's enormous verbal output, one gets the impression that his/her speech is very well developed, but when listening carefully, one notices a sense of being very busy, uninhibited, a monotonous tone and a clear lack of substance, even though the speech is pseudo-adult. Rourke refers to a sort of "cocktail party speech". NLD children speak with very little tone and prose, and seem to rely totally on the left-hand side of the brain. They have a lot of difficulty in sticking a story together and making it comprehensible to the listener. At a very young age one could mistake this for articulation difficulty. However, it usually disappears with time. In reference to this, the term "non-verbal learning disability" seems out of place, because one gets the impression from the name of the condition that nothing is wrong with the child's verbal ability.

The child's phonological aptitude is often well developed. Also, the recording and associative reproduction of information are adequate. Verbal memory is so well developed that the child remembers something exactly as s/he heard in the past. The language problems the child will be faced with are problems related to substance and pragmatics. Spontaneous use of language hardly ever happens, because the child has difficulty bringing new aspects into a conversation. Because the child has trouble using language in a functional way, communication problems often arise. This is a major problem when one knows that language is the child's primary way of communicating, gathering information and reducing fears. A consequence of this is that the child uses repetition when trying to get a point across verbally, because s/he knows no other way.

1.2.6 Emotions

NLD children seem to have difficulty recognizing their own and other people's emotions. They get overrun by emotions and don't know how to deal with them or keep them under control. The capacity to feel an appropriate emotion in a given situation is underdeveloped. For example, the child might laugh in a situation that is not laughable or funny in any way. Or the child may use language without knowing the emotional baggage that some words carry. Also, the child won't understand when someone is saying something emotional.

Physical contact, such as hugging, is something the child has difficulty with. This discomfort with physical contact is often expressed at an early age by tantrums, hyperactivity and destructive tendencies. When the child gets older, this unease is expressed by fear, depression, and being more withdrawn and inhibited. Van der Gaag (Paternotte 2000) tries to clarify this fear within NLD children. He says that their fear comes from the lack of trust they have in their surroundings. Because of the interrupted flow of the information process, they miss out on a lot of information and have difficulty combining the different media of information possible (hearing, seeing, feeling, smelling). The misunderstanding of a situation means that NLD children do not want to make an effort to understand it at all. This is the cause of their insecurity. Their fear is constant, and this can often cause sleeping difficulties.

1.2.7 Social behavior and the ability to adapt

An inactive social life and a lack of insight in social situations are frequent characteristics of NLD children. Their visual–spatial and planning weaknesses have a negative impact on their social interaction. They do not understand non-verbal reactions (signs, facial expressions, body language, the pitch of someone's voice). NLD children also have difficulty estimating the space between themselves and other people, both physically and psychologically, therefore they may attempt to throw themselves into a situation without considering the consequences of their behavior. Sometimes they won't recognize the face of someone they know. The interpretation of subtle aspects of communication, like jokes or signals when one has crossed the line, is very difficult for NLD children.

Behavioral examples of NLD children include standing too close to someone, having difficulty using the correct tone of voice with an adult, and speaking incessantly (a waterfall of words). One of the typical aspects of NLD children is gullibility. They have to make an effort to realize that people can lie, or make sarcastic remarks, or just play them for a fool.

Thompson (1996) makes a good analogy between road signals and non-verbal signals: without road signals, a person can't follow the right direction in traffic. In the same way, NLD children can't understand the world that surrounds them without a basic comprehension of the signs and signals that are used in society. When one considers that more than 65 per cent of human communication is non-verbal, it is clear that NLD children miss out on most of it, or misinterpret a lot of it. This is why they get confused.

NLD children learn very little from reasoning in a situation. Furthermore, approaching and adjusting to a new situation is a difficult task. They prefer to be around people they know, mostly adults, in a familiar situation, with familiar communication. The reason why NLD children prefer speaking with an adult is because adults' answers are easier to predict than those of children. In the playground the adult has a regulating role and that gives the child structure. Structure is very important to the child, so new situations are avoided. The older the child gets, the more uneasy s/he will feel, because s/he does not want to face change or evolution. NLD children try to see things strictly in black and white whereas children without NLD realize, with age, that there's more and more gray.

Functioning in a group is bound to be problematic for NLD children, given their unpredictable behavior and fluctuating activity levels, incessant talking, avoidance of new situations, difficulty in interpreting non-verbal behavior, and diverse problems with tactile information. These are hardly factors that make functioning in a group an easy experience and the child may be rejected. At a later age, in extreme cases, NLD children could have difficulty being in an intimate relationship possibly leading to social isolation.

NLD children are often fearful and insecure. They do not understand the concept of cause and effect, and can have difficulty grasping humor. They will try to simplify another person's behavior by taking one word that person said and responding to that word. Their emotional difficulties are amplified by the fact that it is hard for them to perceive problems and/or insecurities in themselves.

1.3 Progress in school

In this section, we will explore the consequences that NLD characteristics have on the child's scholastic development. Generally, it is difficult to estimate an NLD child's capacities.

When it comes to *technical reading* (word coding) NLD children have difficulty because of the limited capacity they have in making visual–spatial estimations. Analysis of written language is a chore. Due to the fact that they have a well-developed phonological mechanism, their technical reading does get better after long repetitious exercise. They have a good memory for sounds, words and phrases and are capable of audible discrimination, analysis and synthesis. When working in groups (in the fourth or fifth year of primary school), NLD children are able to achieve a decent level of reading, thanks to the writing of letters in relation to their sound when spoken. Reading then becomes a routine activity (left hemisphere of the brain), and so NLD children read very quickly, with very little intonation or punctuation, and a tendency to guess the sound of words (Hakvoort and Thoonen 1999). Ninety-five per cent of their mistakes will be due to the fact that they write words as they sound (I skraipt my nee). Because of their visual limitations they do not realize that the word is spelled incorrectly.

Lack of ability to form concepts is the root cause of the NLD child's failure to understand when reading (Hakvoort and Thoonen 1999). Reading comprehension seems to be and stay a problem for most NLD children. Every text is considered to be new information (right hemisphere of the brain), and reading between the lines to understand the full meaning of the text is a problem.

With mathematics, NLD children have difficulty visualizing a problem in order to solve it. They can't create a concrete representation from numbers. Because of their lack of spatial ability, they find it hard to position the numbers, especially when faced with multi-digit numbers. Arranging numbers in a specific order is something else NLD children have a hard time doing (Jongepier 1999a). They can also be misled when faced with bold print or checkered paper for mathematical exercises.

> When Joyce does mathematical exercises with long columns of sums and subtractions, she often loses track. She puts answers to one question at the end of a different question, or she all of a sudden skips a whole lot of questions and puts the answer somewhere else entirely.

NLD children have a difficult time when it comes to understanding mathematics – subtractions are especially hard. Systematically considering approaches to a problem is also hard, because the child's thoughts have to be systematically arranged. The child does not see a new challenge in a new type of exercise. However, having some kind of automatic system is possible, after a long and repetitive exercise (like learning multiplications by heart). Many NLD children seem to have difficulty with abstract exercises. The child might know the rules needed, but applying them is very hard. Mathematics seems to them like a magic trick. By the end of primary school the mathematical problems are visible in the way the child reasons and in their difficulty when it comes to forming a judgment. Their mathematical weaknesses are expressed in a lack of perseverance, untidiness, confusion when it comes to mathematical signs (multiplication, addition, subtraction and division), and getting the order of digits in a number mixed up.

These last two types of weakness seem to coincide with weak visual coordination.

The NLD child's level in mathematics is lower than in reading and writing, and this is an important factor in diagnosing NLD.

The NLD child's writing is weak because of the difficulty with movement patterns and visual coordination. Remembering the shapes of letters (visual memory) and the right sequence of elements that form a letter is hard for the NLD child, who will always see a letter as several elements brought together, and will have difficulty seeing it as a whole.

> At a certain point, Joyce seemed to have mastered the coordination of separate capital letters. The letters did not take a different shape every time she wrote them down. Once the transition to words and sentences is made, however, Joyce is yet again making mistakes when it comes to the shape and position of the letters. The coordination of three elements – the pattern of each letter, the order of the letters (spelling) and thinking ahead about what she wants to write – gives her great difficulty.

After overcoming the child's visual–spatial weakness and doing a lot of repetitious exercise, flowing legible handwriting is possible. The writing is done in a routine-like manner, and could eventually result in neat handwriting, but it will be done at a very slow speed.

Something that could be quite misleading is the above-average performance of an NLD child when it comes to routine tasks. However, especially in the later years of school, the child could still show problems. For example the child's verbal memory may become less and less reliable, and this will take its toll.

1.4 Etiology

NLD is described as a structural, cerebral-organic condition in the right-hand side of the brain, whereby the so called "white matter" is affected. The white matter is meant to pass on information from within the central nervous system and to combine information of different types together (Eilander 1992). Rourke (1987, in Serlier-van den Bergh *et al.* 1997) suggests that white matter problems are the basis of NLD, and their presence is necessary for NLD to develop. Graauwmans (1995) and Njiokiktijen (1999) suggest that NLD is somehow connected to the problematic functioning of the part of the white matter known as the corpus callosum, a thick band of nerve fiber that connects the two cerebral hemispheres. Not all children have a clearly distinguishable cause for white matter functional problems. Also there is not one specific kind of problem related to white matter. The most likely reason for the existence of a white matter problem is as a result of disturbed brain development, whereby the right side is underdeveloped and the left side is overdeveloped. Although brain scans mostly show a minimal abnormality in the right-hand side, there is usually no overtly clear neurological cause. The developmental disturbance could be the consequence of:

- a shortage of oxygen at birth

- endocrinal factors

- shortage of food in the early years

- external factors such as radiation or an accident (Smeets and Van de Wiel 1996).

The role of possible genetic factors in the appearance of NLD has not yet been proved. It is assumed that the development of

NLD is due to a cerebral-organic disturbance and not the consequence of a dysfunctional family life or poor education.

When it comes to white matter problems, Rourke has two theoretical principles:

- the more dysfunctional the white matter is, the bigger the chance that NLD is present

- the earlier white matter dysfunctions occur, the more likely it is that there will be interrupted development in the building and structure of both cerebral hemispheres.

In fact, the right-hand side of the brain shows more white matter than the left-hand side and the effect of the white matter is more considerable in the right-hand side (Graauwmans 1995). Although the right-hand side of the brain is mostly involved with the learning of new things and the left-hand side for routine, automated tasks and fast application of knowledge, the NLD child has great difficulty in learning and understanding new concepts, in processing and integrating different kinds of information.

Of the total pupil population, 10 per cent have learning and/or behavioral disabilities. There is, as yet, very little research into the prevalence of NLD within that group. The available literature is not unanimous on this subject. Thompson (1996) speaks of percentages ranging from 1 to 10. Serlier (in Langelaan 1999) finds that in 10 per cent of children with a learning disability there is a question of NLD. At the Dr Hans Berger Clinic in Breda, 5 per cent of children reported as having a learning disability are eventually diagnosed with NLD (Graauwmans 1995). The number of children who are diagnosed with NLD seems to be increasing. This development is due to the fact that earlier recognition is more and more frequent. The boy/girl ratio is 1:1 (Graauwmans 1995).

1.5 Explanatory model

To explain the complex manifestation of NLD, Rourke (Rourke 1989; Harnadek and Rourke 1994) developed the so-called *brain-behavioral model* (see Figure 1.1). In this model, the development of the brain (neuroanatomical and neuropsychological characteristics) and the development of behavior are brought together. The developmental process of the brain is characterized by primary, secondary and tertiary verbal functions that have common traits. The *primary level,* which according to Rourke forms the basis for NLD, is the level on which the child receives the information: *the perception.* (It must be noted that Rourke only takes audio-visual and tactile aspects into consideration. When thinking involves sensory integration (Ayres 1991) smell, taste, balance and kinesthetic feeling should also be taken into account.)

The way in which information is perceived (through all senses) is essential in making connections between the different pieces of information. This can be seen in the *second level: the level of attention* of Rourke's model. The way in which connections are made in the brain has consequences for the anchoring and integrating of information particles in the *memory: the tertiary level.* Shortages in the primary level have their effect on the secondary level which in turn has its effect on the third and verbal levels.

Summary:

Primary:	Perception:	Receiving information
Secondary:	Attention:	Connection of information
Tertiary:	Memory:	Integration of information

Together, these neurological developmental problems influence the child's behavior, their scholastic proficiencies and their ability to adjust their socio-emotional skills.

Neuropsychological brain-behavioural model of the NLD syndrome
B. P. Rourke (1989)

Diagnostic Criterion 1
atypical neuropsychological profile

Brain

Neuropsychological Skills

1. **Primary Level: Perception**

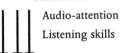

   Audio-perception

   Simple psychomotor

   Exploration of known material

2. **Secondary Level: Attention**

   Audio-attention

   Listening skills

Neuropsychological Shortcomings

1. **Primary Level: Perception**

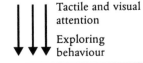

   Visual-spatial

   Tactile perception

   Complex psychomotor

   Exploration of new things

2. **Secondary Level: Attention**

   Tactile and visual attention

   Exploring behaviour

3. **Tertiary Level: Memory**

Audio-memory

Verbal memory

3. **Tertiary Level: Memory**

Tactile and visual memory

Concept-understanding

Abstract thought

Problem solving

4. **Verbal Level**

Phonology

Reception

Memory and repetition

Association

Quantity of verbal information

4. **Verbal Level**

Articulation

Intonation

Verbal coordination

Content

Grammatical construction

Functional speech

1-4 of the neuropsychological skills are all an influence on scholastic skills (5a) and socio-emotional and adaptive skills

1-4 of the neuropsychological shortcomings are all a socio-emotional influence on scholastic shortcomings (5b)

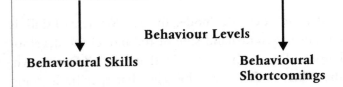

Behaviour Levels

Behavioural Skills

Behavioural Shortcomings

Diagnostic Criterion 2
atypical didactic profile

5a. Scholastic Skills

Written coordination (automatic, end of primary school)

Word decoding

Spelling

Phonetic memory

5a. Scholastic Shortcomings

Written coordination (needs to be taught)

Reading comprehension

Technical and mathematics

Algebra

Exact sciences

Diagnostic Criterion 3
Socio-emotional and adaptive deficiencies

5b Adaptive and socio-emotional skills

Not shown

5b Adaptive and socio-emotional skills

Ability to adjust in new situations

Social competence

Emotional stability

Activity level

Figure 1.1 Neuropsychological brain-behavioural model of the NLD Syndrome

On the left-hand side of the model, the development of skills is reflected. On the right-hand side of the model the developmental process for the characteristics that form NLD is shown. From the NLD model, it can be seen that specific learning disabilities and a shortage of social skills do not have a direct connection to the central nervous system, but can be understood as being independent variables of neuropsychological shortages on levels 1–4.

From research into the stronger and weaker sides of NLD children, on a socio-emotional level one finds many shortcomings. The research has (as yet) found no socio-emotional skills in these children. However, from our experiences within the school, we feel that the inability to adapt in familiar situations and the extreme sensitivity to conditioning in this area can be improved.

From Rourke's model, there are three diagnostic criteria to be deduced (Serlier *et al.* 1997). First, there has to be an *atypical neuropsychological profile* in combination with certain skills and deficiencies that come to light in the child's expressions (diagnostic criterion 1). Second, there have to be indications of an *atypical didactical profile* in connection with skills and scholastic performance (diagnostic criterion 2). *Specific shortcomings in the socio-emotional and adaptive functioning* of the child are the third factor (diagnostic criterion 3).

CHAPTER 2

Characteristics of NLD

Non-verbal learning disabilities are still, in many cases, insufficiently recognized and understood. Parents and teachers who express concern at an early stage are often told by professionals that their child is just a perfectionist, or that their child is just immature or clumsy and simply behaves a little differently to other children of his/her age. Often the case only gets taken seriously when the child's scholastic performance starts to deteriorate. The early medical history of the child may point to the possibility of NLD. Characterizing aspects of the young NLD child include:

- slower than average development of language and coordination

- a lack of exploration

- fear of new situations

- a slowly developing sense of self-sufficiency
  (Rourke in Serlier-van den Bergh *et al.* 1997).

NLD children experience interrupted development. They may forget skills that seemed to be under control. The most obvious NLD characteristics begin to come to the fore between the ages of 7–8 and then manifest themselves very clearly between the ages of 10–14. These characteristics are most obvious in adulthood.

The goal of this chapter is to give an overview of two developmental profiles of NLD children that could prove useful to teachers, pediatricians, psychologists and parents to help them trace and identify possible signs of NLD. The reason these profiles have been included in their entirety is because they are the most concrete and frequent in the appearance of NLD.

The developmental profiles may slightly overlap. It is important to mention that not all aspects of NLD are as strongly recognizable as others; every child is an individual and as such has an individual profile (Jongepier 1999a).

2.1 Palombo's developmental profile

Palombo (1994) delivers a developmental profile with signs in early development that could *possibly* point to the presence of NLD. The described profile is sectioned into a number of phases that lead up to the third year of primary school.

Baby

If a baby does not communicate with the parent by smiling, and is passive and hardly shows any desire to explore, then the parent should consider the likelihood of NLD.

Baby–toddler (1–2 years old)

At this age, visual–spatial and coordination problems are visible: the child is clumsy, has difficulty coordinating movement (balance) and has great difficulty managing toys and putting together simple puzzles. The child learns slowly, and warnings and instructions have to be endlessly repeated by the educator. The child's reactions to correction show signs of frustration and anger. Self-sufficiency is under-developed.

Toddler (from the age of 3)

The toddler's speech is difficult to understand because of articulation problems. These will disappear quite soon and the strong verbal side will come to light. The child does not know how to play with other children. The child is very demanding towards the educator and often shows signs of separation anxiety.

Kindergarten (4–6 years old)

At this age NLD children are smart and verbally very well developed, but their behavior lags behind. Bigger problems may arise when they are in contact with their peers. In the laying of their educational foundation in kindergarten, initial problems with reading are recognizable as well as illegible handwriting. Simple mathematical exercises are also difficult. Educators find NLD children at this stage hard to handle and assess, and get the feeling that they are constantly correcting, punishing and limiting the child. They find it hard to understand why the child will throw a tantrum when they do what they think the child will consider fair. The family life in its entirety revolves around the NLD child.

Primary school (from the age of 7)

Between the ages of 7–8, NLD shows itself in all its facets. This is usually when it is recommended to parents/educators that they look into diagnosis and treatment.

2.2 Thompson's developmental profile

Thompson developed a profile that allows for NLD to be recognized and discovered. From her practical experience with NLD children she has formulated a number of characteristics that are typical but, again, do not figure in every NLD child. The described development through middle school until adulthood might at first glance seem less relevant to basic education, so it should be considered together with the option of a special school or treatment. The advantage with this profile is that it is good to know which concrete developments and problematic aspects to expect in the future. The list shown below could be used as a checklist. It must be noted that the age-sectioning accords with the US educational system and does not completely coincide with the British one.

Baby–toddler (0–6 years old)

- No visible developmental retardation, with the exception of psychomotor coordination.

- No exploration.

- Language and speech develop early.

- All objects get a verbal label.

- Drunk-like manner when attempting to walk.

- Does not automatically regain balance after being picked up.

- Holds on to anything or anyone to maintain balance.

- Bumps into things.

- Remarkably good verbal memory (exact).

- Reading and recognizing letters and numbers develops early.

- Sees everything in black and white.

- Takes everything literally.

- Weak physical coordination: prefers eating and playing on the floor.

- Balance problems: difficulty riding a tricycle.

- Coordination problems and lack of visual-spatial insights: fear of heights.

- Difficulty with simple movements: throwing and catching a ball, standing on one foot, kicking a ball, climbing, jumping.

- Does not like building-construction materials, prefers board games that require spelling/reading (Scrabble/Monopoly).

- Lack of refined coordination: does not want to eat with cutlery and has difficulty tearing, sticking and coloring.

- Difficulty getting dressed (buttons, zippers, putting clothes on backwards or inside-out).

- Problems with change and new situations like getting used to kindergarten.

- Considered as talented by parents and teachers.

- Avoids spontaneous social interaction, often has one best friend.

- Difficulty stopping an activity.

Primary school (6–10 years old)

- If no diagnosis has taken place, the child could be in an "enrichment program for talented children".

- Difficulty following instructions that consist of going through several steps.

- Slow worker.

- Does not apply knowledge in new situations.

- Loses interest when attention needs to be focused on work.

- Problems with coordination that are visible in the child's handwriting, when cutting something, when tying shoelaces or inserting a key into a door.

- Talks him/herself through tasks at hand.

- Talks incessantly.

- Difficulty making partitions on a sheet of paper and writing numbers down in a vertical row.

- Difficulty copying from the blackboard where a combination of vertical and horizontal elements is required; often the imaginary left-hand side margin keeps shifting to the right.

- Writing exercises require a lot of effort and are very slow.

- Spelling mistakes are of a phonetic nature.

- Difficulty with cursive handwriting because diagonals are perceived with more difficulty.

- Difficulty reading a watch.

- Takes everything literally and is therefore thought to be slow and not very sharp.

- Continuously makes wrong estimations and interpretations.

- Difficulty adapting to a replacement teacher.

- Trusts people naively.

- Seen as strange or weird by his/her peers.

Middle school (11–14 years old)

- Often gets excluded and teased.

- Misunderstood by pupils and teachers.

- Difficulty acting his/her own age.

- Trouble with studying and homework; often wrongly accused of having a lack of motivation and laziness.

- Visual-spatial inability: getting lost in school, slow in moving from one classroom to another, difficulty fitting things into his/her locker.

- Difficulty understanding graphs and tables.

- Emotional instability (depression) as a consequence of not being able to live up to the expectations of his/her peers.

- Takes everything literally and has difficulty understanding abstract concepts, figurative speech, analogies and idioms.

- Grades considerably lower than in primary school.

High school (15–18 years old)

- Acceptance from peers increases; often has one or two good friends.

- When an adequate remedial or compensation program is applied, performance improves considerably; on the other hand, dropping-out could occur.

- Still thinks in concrete literal terms.

- Little interaction with the opposite sex.

- Problems with his/her first job.

- Difficulty learning how to drive.

- Socially immature, therefore labeled as "weird" or "a nerd".

- Low self-esteem.

Adulthood

- Has a job that is below his/her education/intelligence level.

- Problems at work; supervisors have to explain and demonstrate.

- Intimate relationships are difficult, understanding non-verbal signals is hard.

- Gets caught in relationship-related problems.

- Relies too much on literal, exact memories.

- Dysfunctions rooted in NLD get worse.

- Periods of depression, sometimes followed by schizophrenia.

When, based on observations of a child, suspicions of NLD arise, a diagnostic consultation can give more clarity. In the next chapter, we take a closer look at diagnosis.

CHAPTER 3

Diagnosing NLD

In practice, parents of NLD children might be given a very different diagnosis to NLD even though the children all fit into the NLD spectrum (Van de Vlugt, in Paternotte 1998). A couple of examples of applied terms within the diagnosis, which each accentuate a different aspect of NLD, are:

- *right-hand hemisphere syndrome*: the right side of the brain functions less well, whereby the processing of global, new, complex and spatial information is problematic

- *white matter deficiency*: an irregularity in the protective layer (white matter) around the nerve vessels that makes it harder for information to get through. As the right-hand side of the brain has more of this matter, its functions are affected

- *prefrontal syndrome*: the less than adequate functioning of the front part of the brain, which has a consequence mostly on higher functions such as motivation, organizational skills and planning

- *disharmony profile:* substantial difference between verbal skills and performance skills, the latter being the weakest.

It is important to realize that there are many levels of NLD. As emphasized earlier, not every NLD child has all the characteristics of NLD. To get a well-balanced diagnosis, a consultation is necessary using the proper instruments. Follow-up consultations are also necessary, because of the changing nature of NLD with age. In Section 3.1 a few instruments used in diagnosing NLD are cited. Section 3.2 contains introductory information on the relationship of NLD to other learning and developmental difficulties.

3.1 Instruments used for diagnosis

Hellemans (1995) gives a review of the instruments that, when used in conjunction with each other, give a clear diagnosis. In the *anamnesis conversation with the parents* of the child – an important part of the diagnosis when a preliminary case history is established – one can deduce whether the child in question has the typical characteristics of NLD. Rourke's overview, as described in Chapter 1 (Figure 1.1) can be helpful. Hendriksen, Vles and Ma (1998, in Hendriksen 1999) are especially tuned in when it comes to analyzing the relevant information. They focus on the stages that feature in the development of skills, a discrepancy in visual-spatial and verbal functioning, and the difficulty and/or fear the child experiences when faced with new situations.

The *Child Behavior Checklist* (CBCL) and *Teacher Report Forms* (TRF) (Achenbach 1993) can offer a clear view on the presence of ADHD-like behavior (in younger children) or internalizing problems (in older children). In the *profile of school developments,* attention must be paid to a combination of relatively good performance in technical reading and spelling, phonologically accurate spelling mistakes, and weak performance in mathematics and reading comprehension. Harnadek and Rourke (1994) emphasize that one must always look at reading and spelling performance in comparison to mathematical performance and not look at either in isolation. Furthermore, a neuropsychological intelligence consultation can give information relating to typical NLD characteristics in the areas of intelligence profiling, coordination skills, audiovisual and tactile information processing, language skills, memory functions, and the abilities to form concepts and solve problems. From *observations* during the neuropsychological testing, information can be gathered about social skills, perseverance, verbal output and ways of exploration. From a *neurological consultation*, possible signs of dysfunction in the brain can be shown.

Figure 3.1 shows which neuropsychological testing option delivers results on specific NLD characteristics.

NLD Characteristic	Research instrument
Disharmonious intelligence profile (VIQ minimum of 10–15 points higher than FIIQ)	WISC-RN: Block patterns and images very low RAKIT: Weak writing skills
Interrupted processing of tactile information, finger agnosis, dysfunctional graphesthesis, disrupted stereognosis, especially on the left side of the brain.	Recognition by touching with fingers, recognizing number or letter written on the fingertips.
Weak complex psychomotor.	Grooved Pegboard Test. Finger Tapping. Imitation of complex positions.

Visual information processing is weak, perception of structure is weak.	WISC-RN: Incomplete signs, patterns, putting cards in the right order.
	Trail making test.
	Rey complex figures.
	Beery-VMI.
	Bicycle drawing (Kold and Wishaw).
Weak visual memory.	Testing of visual-perception skills.
	Rey complex figure test.
Insufficient audio-information processing.	TvK Discrimination.
	TvK Synthesis.
Simple language skills relatively good.	WISC-RN: Vocabulary, Information TvK.
Weak language skills when complex material is involved.	WISC-RN: Maths and Understanding.
	TvK Hidden Meanings.
Good verbal memory, difficulty solving non-verbal problems, forming of concepts, learning from feedback.	WISC-RN: Maths category test.
	Tactual performance test.

Figure 3.1 Effects of neuropsychological testing on specific NLD characterisitcs

Based on multiple studies, Rourke (1999) concludes that in the *WISC-RN intelligence profile of children with NLD*, in 76 per cent of the cases one finds:

- the highest scores within the verbal section in two of the three subtests Information, Conjunctions and Vocabulary

- the lowest scores within the performance section in two of the three performance subtests Patterns, Figure laying and Substitution.

According to Rourke, these findings can be used as useful guidelines when judging the intelligence profile.

Hendriksen, Vles and Ma (1998, in Hendriksen 1999) do not research the intelligence profile with the WISC-RN, but with the Kaufman *Assessment Battery for Children* (K-ACB). They see the discrepancy between the potential in sequential information processing (left side of the brain) and the ability to do simultaneous information processing (right side of the brain) as a confirmation of the atypical intelligence profile in NLD children.

The disharmony in the intelligence profile is not as clearly recognizable in younger children (Serlier-van den Bergh 1999). Throughout primary school (6–10 years old) the NLD child's relatively high level of verbal skills becomes more evident. With less gifted children with NLD the difference between their verbal and visual-spatial skills seems to be less extreme. Serlier-van den Bergh (in Paternotte and Serlier-van den Bergh 2000) emphasizes that finding a difference between verbal and visual-spatial intelligence is not a concluding factor in the diagnosis of NLD. It shows, however, that further consultation and research is necessary. With NLD one needs to realize that it is a combination of subtest scores that characterizes the intelligence profile. The special school De Hondsberg in Oisterwijk has a publication about the use of WISC-RN in diagnosis (Serlier-van den Bergh, Schaaijk and Van der Vlugt 2000).

At the De Hondsberg school, research was undertaken into the usability of the (then still experimental) *Non-verbal Learning Disability Scale* in differentiating children with and without

NLD. *De NLD-schaal* (Serlier-van den Bergh *et al.* 1997) is a translation of *the NLD scale: experimental version* (1993), that Rourke put together from empirical characteristics of children with NLD. The group the NLD-scale focuses on is 7–17-year-olds. During this period, patterns of neuro-cognitive and socio-emotional change can be perceived. The scale is an observation instrument that is made up of two parts, with questions that are completely independent from each other. These are asked of a few educators (teachers, classroom assistants, group leader, mentor, parent/caretaker) and answered on a three-point scale. The first part contains questions about neuropsychological symptoms, while the second part analyses didactical and socio-emotional skills.

During the research at De Hondsberg (1997) the scale was applied to 24 mentally handicapped children, half of whom were diagnosed with NLD. To be a part of this group, the children had to match up to three criteria:

- an atypical neuropsychological profile

- an atypical didactical profile. (The verbal achievements of the child will be a minimum of 10 points stronger than other academic achievements. The visual-spatial and psychomotor deficiencies, as well as the didactical age equivalent for mathematics, will be a minimum of 5 points lower than the didactical age equivalent for reading/spelling.)

- deficiencies in socio-emotional and adaptive characteristics.

The NLD scale was used at two different times for all the children (with a six-week gap in between). During the first series, the scale did not differentiate the children with NLD.

During the second series, it did. From the research, it can be deduced that teachers and classroom assistants are the most consistent at various stages in recognizing NLD characteristics. Also, there is a strong convergence within the pairings of teacher-classroom assistant and mentor-group leader. The researcher found that, based on the findings, there was hope for the future use of the NLD scale, although the factor discriminating between NLD and neurotypical children was insufficient at the time. The applicability and usefulness of the scale are minimal when the judges do not agree sufficiently. There has to be some degree of convergence of opinion as to whether certain combinations of skills and shortcomings that fit the NLD spectrum are present.

The construction of a renewed version of the NLD-scale, the also experimental *Nederlandse NLD-schaal* (Dutch NLD scale), has been applied in many studies with a large pupil population (including students from special schools). The De Brug special school participated in the research of the De Hondsberg school in March 1999. A number of students, parents and teachers filled in the NLD scale and recent information about intelligence and didactical progress was gathered. The results show the degree to which it can be assumed that these children have NLD. When a couple or several characteristics of NLD appear, specific neuropsychological consultation is necessary. At the moment (2000–2002), progress is being made with regard to normalizing, and improving the reliability and validity of the NLD scale (Serlier-van den Bergh 1999), in the hope of using the scale on larger and more diverse populations (6–12-year-olds with average or below average levels of intelligence). The point is to be able to make a quicker and more preemptive diagnosis. Serlier-van den Bergh is hoping to promote this research in the autumn of 2000.

3.2 NLD in relation to other learning and developmental difficulties

The diagnosis of NLD does not use a classification system based on clinical, behavioral observations (like the DSM-IV and ICD-9). The novelty and independence of NLD (from other diagnoses) is not exactly clear. Furthermore, there is a question as to whether NLD may be considered a syndrome. An important discussion point is whether NLD has a collection of characteristics that are clearly different from other developmental difficulties or if NLD has characteristics that overlap with other known developmental difficulties, the only difference being that these characteristics are described from a non-clinical point of view, namely neuropsychology. Van der Gaag (in Paternotte 2000) still sees NLD as a thinking model that could be useful to understand children better and to get clearer insight into a better treatment, by finding what the strengths and weaknesses of the child are.

NLD – a term that emphasizes information-processing more than behavioral patterns – is characterized by a typical neuropsychological profile that could coincide with, and in a certain way resemble, various diverse psychiatric ailments in children. Rourke (1995, in Hendriksen 1999) has developed the following hierarchy whereby he posits a connection between NLD and neurological ailments in which the white matter plays a part.

Level 1

Many ailments show the characteristics of NLD, and some coincide with it: Asperger Syndrome, Williams Syndrome, hydrocephalus, right-hemisphere damage and incomplete development of the corpus callosum.

Level 2

The majority of children with the following ailments show many of the traits found in NLD: amongst others, acute lymphatic leukemia and fetal alcohol syndrome.

Level 3

Children with the following disabilities show some traits of NLD: among them, traumatic brain damage and multiple sclerosis.

Based on the distinctions shown above, a diagnosis of NLD is often (but not always) paired with developmental problems in terms of behavior (Asperger Syndrome) and in a neurological sense (hydrocephalus). This does not make a differential diagnosis any easier. NLD should be separated from ADHD, disabilities within the autistic spectrum (autism, Asperger Syndrome, PDD-NOS), mental retardation, deafness, hard of hearing, Williams Syndrome, serious emotional difficulties, dyscalculia, dysgraphia, hyperlexia, dyspraxia and coordination developmental problems. In the sections that follow, NLD is compared with the above-mentioned ailments. They examine, using the available literature, the possible characteristics that separate NLD from other psychiatric ailments in children.

ADHD

At an early age, NLD children are often considered to have ADHD. This is due to the fact that they show signs of hyperactivity, impulsive behavior and problems handling a multitude of visual stimuli. The hectic behavior that has its roots in weakly developed tactile skills, is known to reach its peak at the age of 4–5 years old, and quickly diminishes from then on. Furthermore, this lack of attention will limit itself to only one developmental area. With ADHD there is question of a combination of hyperactivity, impulsiveness and a short attention span that manifests itself in all developmental areas for a longer period. The type of information missed because of ADHD is wide-ranging – visual, tactile, audio and verbal. The information that bypasses an NLD child is mostly of a visual and tactile nature (Van de Vlugt, in Paternotte 1998). ADHD and NLD can coexist though. The clinical image of ADHD with a child who has NLD could then possibly have been created by a right-hemisphere dysfunction or a frontal dysfunction.

Autism

The neuropsychological profile of children who have autism looks completely different to that of children with NLD. In particular, it is the higher performance IQ than verbal IQ, and relatively strong visual-spatial skills, that separate the autistic child from the NLD child. The typical left-hemisphere hypothesis for autism is the complete opposite to the typical right-hemisphere hypothesis for NLD (Klin *et al.* 1995; Klin and Volkmar 1997). Furthermore, the source of these ailments within the brain is known to be different. In children with NLD, the problem is created by white matter damage in between the hemispheres (Rourke 1989), whereas autism is primarily the consequence of white matter damage *within* the (left) hemisphere.

Asperger Syndrome

Noticeable characteristics of children with Asperger Syndrome are strong verbal use of language skills and a monotonous tone of voice; these are things they have in common with NLD children (Graauwmans 1997). Many children with Asperger

Syndrome have a neuropsychological profile that is comparable to the profile of NLD children who have a verbal intelligence that is significantly more developed than their overall performance intelligence. Van der Gaag (in Paternotte 2000) says that nine out of ten children with NLD have Asperger Syndrome. The common factor seems to be problems in the right hemisphere of the brain (Klin *et al.* 1995; Klin and Volkmar 1997). The opposite does not seem to apply – as can be deduced from Rourke's hierarchy, a small number of children with NLD do not have Asperger Syndrome. Further research should show how these syndromes differ. A possible separating characteristic could be the fact that a child with Asperger Syndrome does not have a serious problem with mathematical exercises. Brumback, Harper and Weinberg (2000) conclude that Asperger Syndrome could possibly be a more serious form of NLD, where hyper-emotional behavior and hyper-dysprosodia are at the forefront.

Clearly, there are various opinions as to the relationship between NLD and Asperger Syndrome, so there are not (as yet) any clear differential diagnostics.

Dyscalculia

When faced with children who have problems with mathematics, one must be wary of giving a diagnosis of NLD too quickly (Ruijssenaars and Ghesquiere 1999). Dyscalculia is not the only problem of an NLD child. There are also language problems and shortcomings in other areas. Furthermore, with NLD the relationship between weak mathematical skills and relatively well developed reading and spelling skills need to be thoroughly studied before anything can be concluded.

Deafness/hard of hearing

Because of the slow development of speech in NLD children, the possibility of deafness can be tested for by audiological research at quite an early stage (Dumont 1994). When these children eventually start to talk, their speech and language should develop at a higher pace than the average child, and limitations in hearing can then be ruled out.

Mental retardation

Because of the NLD child's limited urge to explore at a young age and slow development of speech, one could suspect mental retardation (Dumont 1994). The fast pace at which the verbal side catches up, however, rules out this hypothesis. Children with NLD generally have an average intellectual capacity and mostly do not have a mental handicap. The fact that a lower than average intelligence level can occur in NLD children as well makes diagnosis even harder.

Hyperlexia

In some cases, NLD may appear to be paired with hyperlexia. This syndrome, which reveals itself at a young age (between 18 months and 5 years old), is characterized by a remarkable fascination with letters, numbers, patterns and symbols, and also very premature reading, writing, spelling and mathematical skills. Hyperlexia can be separated into two subtypes (Richman 1997): on the one hand, the variant that overlaps autistic-like traits and a language disability; and on the other hand, the variant that overlaps visual-spatial coordination problems and Asperger-like characteristics. The supposition is that NLD can be a part of hyperlexia as far as visual-spatial and coordination problems are concerned (see Figure 3.2).

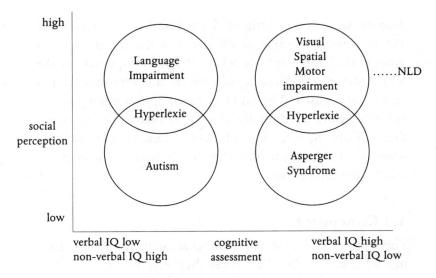

Figure 3.2 Types of Hyperlexie (Richman 1997)

Williams Syndrome (or Williams-Beuren Syndrome)

Children with Williams Syndrome seem to have a lot in common with NLD children (Grejtak 1998; De Kock and Eilander 1994), as a consequence of damage to the connecting channels in the brain. Verbal skills are considerably better developed than other skills. In both types of children, verbal and audio memory seem to function well and technical reading skills and verbal expression are strong. Remarkably, there is a typical type of speech associated with both – "cocktail party speech". Those skills that are weakly developed in children with NLD and Williams Syndrome are logical reasoning or reasoning in an abstract way, the understanding of numbers, and the processing of non-verbal information. Also, both groups can suffer from a short concentration span. A significant difference between Williams Syndrome and NLD children is the fact that Williams Syndrome children say things of some substance, whereas NLD children usually speak in a droning way, saying little of depth (De Kock and Eilander 1994). Another significant difference is the social life both groups of children lead (Grejtak 1998). As opposed to the NLD child, the Williams Syndrome child is very socially and externally focused. The NLD child who, at a young age, is verbally strong and friendly, retreats at a later age. An aspect that Williams Syndrome and NLD children have in common, however, is the difficulty they both have in processing non-verbal information.

3.3 Conclusion

This chapter gave information on what can be found in today's literature about the differences between NLD and other learning/developmental difficulties. Clearly, in the field of differential diagnostics, more research is necessary.

NLD is considered a neuropsychological diagnosis that can possibly be confirmed neurologically (noticeable right-hemisphere dysfunction). Hellemans (1995) suggests making a diagnosis on several levels, for example on a behavioral level (Asperger Syndrome) and at the same time on a neuropsychological level (NLD). Further research should provide more insight into the connection between several diagnoses. The diagnostic research into NLD is still in its early stages.

Although NLD is not an official classification, it can be used as a working hypothesis from which an approach to treatment can be determined. Chapter 4 focuses on the treatment of NLD children.

Treatment of NLD

The diagnosis and treatment of NLD are both still at very early stages. Hakvoort and Thoonen (1999) emphasize that general advice regarding children with NLD is hard to give. The variation in seriousness of the problem is one of the reasons. Despite the uniqueness of every NLD child that makes a general treatment impossible, there are a few focal points that are of importance when treating him/her. Rourke (1993b) and Thompson (1997b) both draw from constant feedback throughout therapy, and stress that letting NLD children know what they can and cannot do is of the utmost importance. Making the most of the strong points and working on the weak points is key. Observing the child in new situations and *not* basing opinions on what the child says (Cracco 1993) provides teachers and parents with the most information about possible adjustment problems, and an intervention strategy can be applied. Rourke (1989, in De Kock and Eilander 1994) says that it is important to know the exact time that the white matter problem arose in order to choose the most effective treatment. If the NLD exposes itself early on in development, it is proposed that stimulating the areas that are deficient is the best thing to do. However, if the NLD manifests itself at a later stage, then the emphasis should be on compensation strategies.

Also, when the NLD has not manifested itself clearly in young children, but work is being done from this hypothesis, there are important guidelines for the treatment, which are described below. Different treatment strategies are appropriate in the classroom and at home.

4.1 Treatment strategies in the classroom

In the organization of classes, the specific skills and limitations of the NLD child can be taken into account in several ways. Bachot and Konig (1999) emphasize that adjustment of the surroundings is the first requirement, before thinking of compensating measures and the training of weak skills. The consequence of the disability need to be made lighter, so that the child will have an easier time in situations to come. A safe environment is the basis for further exploration and development. The classroom organization, the pedagogical-didactic climate and the learning matter demand adjustments when an NLD child is part of a group of children being taught. In paragraphs 4.1.1–4.1.3 these three factors come to light consecutively. Another is illustrated from the treatment experiences with Joyce.

Surely when a teacher in a special school has a classroom with children who have a wide range of disabilities, adjusting the lesson plan is not too difficult? Even if only the main guidelines are applied, it makes the world of difference to an NLD child.

4.1.1 The organization of classes

A classroom with few visual stimuli, which is not too big and open, is a good working environment for a child with NLD. An environment completely based on non-verbal signs is not recommended. Verbal labels could help the child orientate him/herself. A permanent seating place gives the child an overview of the room. In order not to confront the child with his/her visual-spatial limitations, s/he should not be expected to go back and forth to get items s/he needs. If the child has lessons in another part of the school (remedial or other), it might be handy to give him/her a map of the school. This way s/he will not feel too lost in the maze of corridors, stairwells, doors and walls. To appoint another child as a partner in guiding the NLD child through the school is another alternative. Generally, changing classrooms or teachers for a specific lesson should be avoided.

One must take into account that for the NLD child it is very hard to keep a drawer or locker in a useable state. A helping hand while packing away his/her things might give the child a feeling of relief. When helping the child, guide him/her verbally, or label the items that need to be put away at the end of the day. Items that won't fit in the child's drawer or locker should be stored somewhere central in the classroom.

To keep the child's day as predictable as possible, a daily schedule is recommended. In addition, a picture system that is verbally supported by written labels describing the activities illustrated could be useful. In transitional stages (e.g. from work to play; from mathematics to language) the child will require some time to adjust both physically and psychologically to the new situation.

> While treating Joyce, an attempt was made to keep in the same space as much as possible. Within this space, the table layout never changed, and Joyce always sat to the left of the teacher. She also would always sit on the same chair. When entering the classroom there was always a "ritual" that was followed: put the "do not disturb" sign up, switch on the light and take a seat. When, for some reason, the usual classroom could not be used, Joyce was told as soon as the

teacher picked her up from her usual class, and the different room would be made to look as much like the usual one as possible.

4.1.2 The pedagogical-didactical climate

In the treatment of a child with NLD, maximal predictability, making preparations for new situations, applying external structure with sufficient challenges within, and incorporating a lot of training and repetition are absolutely necessary (even when it looks as if the child understands the subject matter). A more instrumental approach, based on the empathic ability of the teacher, is a good starting point for the guidance of an NLD child. The basic attitude of the teacher should be characterized by a constant search for a balance between keeping his/her distance and showing empathy.

Many of these pedagogical points are not only applicable to children with NLD. Other children could benefit from this approach too.

> To keep the treatment predictable for Joyce, a concrete structure was maintained. For every activity undertaken during the hour of treatment, there was a card. The cards look like pictograms where the main activity is described in one word (a combination of visual and verbal aspects). It was made very clear to Joyce that with every main activity came sub-activities. For activities like reading, writing, maths, handwork (visual-spatial), talking, playing, and drawing, there were separate cards. Every card had three dimensions that made it recognizable for Joyce: picture, text, color. Maths was blue, reading was red, writing was green, and handwork was pink. Talking, playing, drawing and book reading were yellow, to emphasize that they were not work, but relaxing/entertaining.
>
> The activity cards were introduced by laying them out on the table from left to right. Then we would decide

together in which sequence the activities would be done. Joyce was actively involved in the choosing and naming of the activities. Every time an activity finished, Joyce asked "And what are we going to do next?". The card for the activity that was just done was put somewhere else in the classroom so that visually-spatial the task was also over. When she sat at her desk again, she crossed out the last activity on a checklist. Next, Joyce was asked "And what is the next activity?", while pointing at the next card. The card was taken out of the row, and placed in front of her and so forth.

This way, Joyce could see precisely how many tasks she still had to do before relaxation, in the form of playing, drawing, or reading a book, and she also knew how long there was to go before she had to return to her classroom.

With Joyce, the following structure was given to her activities:

- Basic rule: first talk, then work. (At the beginning of every hour of treatment, Joyce is reminded of this rule while laying out the card that says "talking".)

- Then, two tasks (the combination varies every hour of treatment she gets); and then, the possibility to relax.

- And yet again, two tasks (again, the combination varies).

The checklist went with the cards but could be used independently. It consisted of a vertical sheet, with a couple of boxes that related to the number of activities finished during the hour of treatment. At the top was written "What have I already done?" Whenever an activity was completed, a box gets crossed out to give an overview, to keep Joyce involved and to give her a positive feeling when the activity was over. During the course of the year, the checklist was left behind, on Joyce's initiative, because she felt the cards gave her enough structure.

Because of the highly developed speech of NLD children, they can be very demanding. As a teacher, one must be careful to keep the amount of conversation under control. Accept that the child asks a lot of questions. S/he finds out about the world's form and content through verbal exploration, although sometimes the questions show a lack of coherence. Try to challenge the child into exploring using different ways besides audio and verbal (sight, touch, smell, taste, kinesthetic feeling, balance). This way, important processes in the cognitive development (object-realization, decentralizing, concept-formation) are helped at the same time.

In every scholastic subject, it is important not to expect any insight, but to sharpen skills by making their use habitual. In a new situation known understandings need to be repeated, because generalization does not happen automatically. The link between a learning situation and quotidian situation must be explicitly and verbally made clear. A realistic attitude is preferable: the teacher must not assume that the child is benefiting fully from the instruction, nor even that s/he understands. Everything that is considered "obvious" for a "normal" child must be explained and structured verbally. Figurative speech should be avoided, as well as irony and abstract comments, unless they are followed by an explanation. The teacher must get used to checking whether the child truly understands, and the child has to be trained to point out what s/he does not understand.

Thompson (1997c) speaks of four basic techniques in educating a child with NLD. First, the teacher must offer *support* to let the child make the most of what is happening in class. A lesson can be discussed beforehand with the child. If s/he is shown a summary of what is to follow, the child will understand more of the lesson. This information can also be given to the child on a computer. Second, Thompson refers to *adjusting*, which includes aspects such as giving the child extra time, avoiding extensive writing exercises, emphasizing quality instead of quantity in writing exercises and focusing on the child's strengths when grading. The third technique is that of forming *parallel activities*. These are activities that follow the lesson plan, but are adjusted to the abilities of the NLD child, such as giving dictation, but using a box with words and letters instead of actually writing them down (see p.76). The last technique is what Thompson calls the *adjusting of expectations*. This is very important. From her experience with NLD children, she has found that they are often overestimated because of their flowing verbal skills and strong aspects in their intelligence profile. As a consequence they try to keep as calm and quiet as possible, because they're afraid they will be "discovered". NLD children benefit from a neutral-positive approach, whereby the background to their negative behavior is researched and alternative ways of dealing with it are found.

4.1.3 The lesson plan

The lesson plan can be subdivided into several specific subject areas. Among them are language, reading, spelling, math, writing, and coordination and developmental lessons to focus visual-spatial skills and socio-emotional development. In the following sections, there are content lists for these lessons. The points of emphasis and adjustment within the education system can be of the utmost importance when a teacher has a child with NLD in his/her classroom.

Language skills

Good language skills will help the child in verbally guiding his/her actions out loud and, at a later stage, just to him/herself (self-instruction). However, support of the other senses must not be forgotten. Visual aids, such as pictograms, can teach the child to have an eye for visual information and not to rely solely on verbal information. While the child learns procedures, s/he can work with verbal rules that describe all the steps that need to be taken. Spelling rules and rules on how to approach a certain type of maths exercise will definitely come in handy. Writing down these rules for the child on a sheet of paper or booklet that is on his/her desk will give the child the opportunity to refer to them. Refinement of the child's language skills can happen through attention to the content (limit the subject matter to a situation) and function (when to say what and how) of his/her language. Learning language through play helps the child with structuring.

In the treatment of Joyce, the refinement of language skills were worked on using the following methods:

1. Developing logical reasoning by asking guiding questions.

2. Telling a story while showing a picture, emphasising the combination of details and structure of the story.

3. Sticking to one subject when talking – when the child changes the subject, ease him/her back to the original one.

4. Bringing empty conversation back to the subject matter at hand, and making the language useful. If this does not work, just cut off the stream of conversation.

5. In certain settings, only discussing matter relevant to the situation. With Joyce, a deal was made that during work, she was only allowed to talk about the work she was doing. If she needed to talk about anything else, there was time for that at the beginning of every hour of treatment, during a break or at the end of the lesson.

6. Letting the child tell a story about something that happened from beginning until end without interruption.

7. Looking at the child when talking to him/her.

At moments of discomfort with the teacher, Joyce has a tendency to start talking about many other different things to avoid the situation. The teacher/therapist will easily be carried away in verbal discussion by arguing with the child. Such discussions must be avoided. The child's attention needs to be redirected by pointing to the page at hand, or by saying with a sigh "you were at this exercise". This will help him/her not to be interrupted by distraction. Also make it clear that this is not the time to be talking because "now, we're working" – this is very effective.

The approach when teaching language skills must be aimed at giving meaning to language and creating connections within stories. This does not mean reading a story to the child.

Reading
Technical reading
When it comes to technical reading, a synthetic sound model is required (Smeets and Van de Wiel 1996) in conjunction with a lot of exercise in sound–sign pairing. This practice should not

be used in a purely audio form, but needs to be visually supported too. An overview of letters or the writing of a letter can be used as a memory support. Furthermore, extra exercises in relation to other aspects of technical reading, such as letter identification and visual discrimination, are recommended. To check whether the child is guessing at the pronunciation of words, interject with questions like, "Is this sentence (grammatically) possible?"

Reading comprehension

To further the child's reading comprehension, the child can be taught to ask him/herself questions about the text. This can be done with the help of a standard list of questions that are placed beside each text. At the PI school an 11-year-old boy had difficulty understanding the content of a text. The teacher made it more understandable by comparing its content to what was happening in the boy's own life and by constantly asking questions while the boy read the text out loud. The questions were expanded, beginning with a simple basic question followed by a more specific question related to detail. The example below shows a question–answer conversation that occurred as a consequence of the sentence, "Mummy went on holiday with Danny and Rose to Granny and Grandpa in Exeter".

Teacher: *When you visit someone, you don't stay home, do you? You leave.*

Child: *Yes, they also went to Exeter.*

Teacher: *Who went to Exeter?*

Child: *Danny and Rose.*

Teacher: *Did Danny and Rose go together, or did someone go with them?*

Child: *Mummy went as well, but actually you can't say*
           they all went to see Granny and Grandpa, because
           they are her parents.

A typical characteristic of this boy with NLD is that he loses himself in the text without the direction of the teacher. After intensive individual guidance, he learnt several strategies that improved his comprehension.

Giving form to text

As a consequence of weak visual-spatial insight, it is quite natural for an NLD child to lose track when faced with a text-heavy page – even more so when there are illustrations involved. For this reason, it is best to avoid pages that are illustrated so that the child can concentrate on the text. Placing a ruler, or even just a finger, under every line of text can focus the child's attention. A dot in the upper left-hand corner of the page helps the child find the beginning of the text more easily.

When the NLD child has developed into a better reader, s/he can offer other weak readers in the group support, by helping them find the right page or assignment, or reading a difficult word. This will not only give the NLD child a sense of independence; s/he will also feel gratified.

Spelling

NLD children, as a consequence of their visual-spatial weakness, do not trust the visual appearances of a word, but rather its sound. While learning how to spell, a strong emphasis must be made on learning both through sound and visuals. Rhymes and songs can help the NLD child remember the form and order of words. Games like word-bingo might be less suitable because of their strong visual nature.

> In the Dutch language, besides the five basic vowels, there are more vowels that are created by putting two or more vowels together. Joyce had some difficulty telling these apart, but with the help of pictograms and some mental shortcuts, she eventually mastered them.

With spelling exercises, the child's weak psychomotor coordination must be taken into account. Copying words from the blackboard – a task that requires a combination of many senses – is extremely hard for the NLD child. It is very important to keep the ultimate goal in mind – spelling, not writing. To make the NLD child write down a word several times is therefore not a solution. Verbal exercises with the help of a tape recorder or working with a box of letters[1] are alternatives when the child has difficulty actually writing.

> Joyce works with the letter box quite regularly. She seems to have a lot of difficulty with the partitions of the box (too many sections) and the small size of the letters. A lot of time is lost looking for the right letter and recognizing it. There are both capital letters and handwritten letters, which does not make it any easier. A smaller box with bigger letters is more efficient for her. Spreading out the letters on the desk is also an option.

With a lot of practice, spelling skills can reach an acceptable level. Spelling is a subject area in which the NLD child can develop quite rapidly. By giving enough attention to the spelling of words that do not read as they sound (e.g. knowing,

---

1   The box of letters: a box that is divided into 26 sections, each section containing little pieces of paper with the appropriate letter. There are capital letters and also handwritten letters.

though, laugh) in the form of repetition, the child will eventually learn the correct spelling. To give the child a chance to be successful, s/he should participate in regular spelling tests with the rest of the class, but obviously with the necessary adjustments (see "Writing" on p.82).

Mathematics

The combination of visual-spatial weakness, psychological coordination problems and weak organizational/planning skills mean that the subject of mathematics is particularly difficult for an NLD child. Choosing the right calculation procedure is a process that requires constant adjustment in order to avoid experiences of failure. Therefore, it is always necessary to keep the child's ultimate goal in mind: learning how to calculate. If the child has difficulty writing down numbers (coordination) an alternative can be found. Attention must always be paid to calculation. Writing down numbers can be practiced another time.

Preparing and beginning mathematics

Before starting work on mathematics, it is important for the child to know the mathematical rules and have a good understanding of numbers. The most effective way for the child to learn the numbers one to ten is to hear the number, see (visual) the illustration of the number, and depict (see) the quantity of that number (Jongepier 1999a).

When it comes to learning about calculation, a procedure of steps, with concrete material and consistant solving strategies, needs to be used. Jongepier (1999a) suggests moving from mechanical calculations towards more functional and insightful calculations. In this train of thought, there appears to be a sequential, step-by-step routine of isolated sums. The structure of the numbers can be made clear by reading the numbers out loud, breaking them down into hundreds, tens and units, or even by playing a memory game.

Choice of method

Methods using visual images of numbers seem to be inappropriate within the special school in Leiden. The NLD child has great difficulty making a link between visual images and numbers. Jongepier (1999a) shows that working with a realistic calculation method is a catastrophe. The child has difficulty in applying past knowledge and understanding presentations within a realistic context. When choosing a calculation method, this has to be taken into consideration. If sums are given in the form of a story, it is a good idea to reduce the amount of irrelevant detail. This way the child can keep him/herself busy transcribing the relevant information, without getting confused.

Use of material

Very few doubt the benefit of visual aids to support mathematical accomplishment. Most scientists (Bachot, Duits and Graauwmans 1996; Smeets and Van de Wiel 1995; Paternotte 1999b; Jongepier 1999a) see this type of aid as very necessary. To broaden the child's insight into mathematics, concrete aids are required – material that is related as closely as possible to technical mathematical proficiency (e.g. a horizontal line of numbers or a mathematical rack). Smeets and Van de Wiel (1996) call the math-box by Van Luit a successful tool for teaching mathematics to children with NLD. Because NLD children have weak psychomotor coordination, the teacher needs to choose material that is manageable. A number-necklace (numerical balls on a string) is something that should be avoided as it is hard for the NLD child to work with. The child's visual-spatial limitation is also relevant when choosing the material. An abacus will be complicated for the child to use, as the movements involved in working it require good coordination and it will only confuse the child (Jongepier 1999a; Paternotte 1999c). The teacher needs to remember that the child will be heavily dependent on the material as s/he has difficulty forming a mental representation of the exercise at hand (Bachot, Duits and Graauwmans 1996; Smeets and Van de Wiel 1996). With more difficult sums, referring to aids seems to be the only way to give the child some insight.

A computer and headphone can be used as support. Working with a computer gives a child motivation and gives variety rather than always working with paper and pen. At a later stage, calculators can be given to the child once s/he has established good basic knowledge.

Strategies of calculation

To give structure to an NLD child's calculation, the best thing to do is to combine the use of mathematical aids with verbally going through the method used to find the solution. The Russian procedure (from aids, with visual and verbal help, to mental images) can then be used. Important calculation rules (algorithms) that are frequent should be written down for the child. Jongepier gives an example (1999a, p.20) of a seven-step plan:

1. Do you know what you have to do?

2. Is your book ready?

3. Begin at the first exercise.

4. Can you get a sum out of it?

5.   Where and how do you write down the answer?

6.   Go over your answers.

7.   Do you know what the next sum is?

Every step has individual focal points, so that the NLD child can work relatively independently. A series of steps such as this can be adjusted to the individual needs of the pupil.

Structure of work-pages

When choosing work-pages, one must try to choose the type with the most simple layout. The paper should have as little color as possible, as few images as possible, and more than enough space to write down the answers. It must be made clear to the child that the exercise may not be changed (it is either + or -). A page may be cut into several parts if it makes the exercise any clearer. The application of frames in between sub-exercises and the placing of arrows can both help in giving structure to the exercise.

> The pages of exercises from Remelka (maths book) are made clearer for Joyce by placing individual exercises in frames. For every exercise, there is a box at the bottom of the frame with the word "done" that can be ticked off whenever the exercise is finished. This gives Joyce both structure and fulfillment. Rows of sums are numbered, so that Joyce tackles the exercises in a systematic fashion and does not skip any exercises. When it is not clear to Joyce where she must write down the answers, little dots are placed next to where the answer should be. Arrows give Joyce direction in going from one exercise to the next. All these adjustments make it easier for Joyce to work more quickly and independently.

For NLD children who have difficulty placing numbers under each other, maths paper can help. Complicated structures such as graphs and tables are best avoided. When the use of graphs and tables is necessary, extensive verbal guidance should be given (not just pointing at them).

When taking all these adjustments into consideration, one can see that the most common methods are not viable options for the NLD child.

Long-term prospects

Some NLD children seem as though they will never acquire basic mathematical skills. They can't seem to do basic exercises involving numbers from one to ten automatically. To them strategies are more like tricks, without any meaningful content.

> Mathematical strategies are hardly picked up by Joyce. She is not able to recognize when a certain strategy needs to be applied. Furthermore, she does not fully understand the strategy. She just puts a verbal label on it and works from verbal memory without checking whether that particular strategy can be applied.

As the child gets older, it has been known for teachers to abandon teaching them more technical mathematics. A conscious choice is made not to enhance the child's mathematical insight. Mostly this happens when it is recognized that the child is still at the mathematical level of a child in the third year of primary school. Attention may then be shifted to the application and learning of tricks, instead of numerical insight. An approach aimed at achieving self-sufficiency in relation to dealing with money, using a calculator and reading a watch takes priority and seems quite successful. From experience, this is a good way to practice number recognition. The NLD child can then look up a page in a book by him/herself and participate in classical class activities (bingo etc.).

Writing

Writing is a process that demands the use of both hemispheres of the brain. The combination of writing skills and planning the content demands the utmost concentration from the NLD child. The formating of ideas about what to write is very difficult as it requires both hemispheres of the brain. Even just starting a writing exercise is extremely hard.

Method of writing

Choosing to write in capitals is an option, although the benefits of this are still being debated. Maintaining a writing pattern takes a lot of effort; just connecting letters is a difficult task. Therefore, a wider handwriting style can help. Emphasizing starting points is another tool that can help. Jongepier (1999a) recommends using lined paper.

> Most types of paper do not give NLD children enough space in between lines, so pages with larger breaks in between lines are recommended. This gave Joyce more room to work with when writing. At a later stage, when Joyce had practiced with narrower lines, the answers were written where they should be. Dots at the beginning of every line indicated where the answers were to go. Sometimes Joyce would not write and just used the box of letters or answered verbally.
>
> Even after a year of treatment, Joyce still needs a lot of structure to maintain a clear overview of a page. Vertical lines indicate when a word has to be copied.

Saying the movement patterns out loud supports systematic writing exercises. In the Dutch exercise book *De Leessleutel* (The

Writing Key) the following explanation is given for the letter
"e": 'when green, go to the side, around, and left around the
corner, all the way down'. Hence, the child makes use of
relatively well developed language skills. Verses for direction
can be made to learn about numbers as well as letters. To make
NLD children comfortable with the visual image of a letter,
pictograms or three-dimensional letter forms can be very
helpful. The speed of most conventional writing methods is
too high for NLD children and they cannot write in between
narrow lines as soon as other children. The transition from
writing individual letters to writing connected ones and then
short sentences is also slower. For the NLD child, it is
important to give attention to the control of separate letters,
first on larger sheets of paper with no lines, and then on smaller
sheets of paper, with wide lines at first and then narrower lines.

> Joyce learned letters and numbers in many ways:
> finger-painting large letters, making small letters out of clay,
> writing in sand, feeling letters in sandpaper, writing in the air.
> These are all exercises that made sure that she maintained
> visual, tactile and coordination familiarity. All the exercises
> were combined with verbal support through saying the
> movement pattern or a letter-story.

Variation can be given by gradually making the lines narrower
and narrower. The computer program called "Mijn eigen
handschrift" (My own handwriting) (Lindeman), that has a
section in capital letters, can be helpful in learning the patterns
of letters. The program requires the use of a mouse, something
someone else will probably have to operate on the NLD child's
behalf at first. There is another computer program, "Spelen met
de muis" (Playing with the mouse), that has been developed to
familiarize the child with the use of a mouse. To make the

keyboard more accessible, special schools in the Netherlands encircle the letters or tape the unnecessary keys down.

Only after the separate letters are mastered can the child attempt to write words. Then, it is recommended that s/he uses paper with wide lines and identified starting points at the beginning of each line. The step from writing words with disconnected letters in between wide lines to writing connected-letter words is considered a leap. When writing a sentence the child has to combine so many tasks (thinking of the sentence, making sure not to make spelling mistakes), that thinking about the shapes of the letters is the least of his/her worries.

> When transferring from writing separate letters to writing full words in between narrower lines, Joyce's coordination took a serious blow. She needed to devote so much attention to the spelling of the words, that there was an increase in rotations and spelling errors. Her writing also no longer stayed in between the lines and instead moved diagonally down the page. Letters that up until now were fine were causing problems. Joyce was conscious of this and became frustrated. Crossing things out, writing quicker and general agitation were the consequences. Therefore, it was decided to take a step back to practicing separate letters, but in between narrower lines.

For practicing writing patterns within narrower lines the Dutch book *Mijn eigen handschrift* (My own handwriting) is suitable. In the book, writing patterns must be inserted into a white horizontal column without going into the blue area that surrounds the column.

Long-term prospects

One may wonder whether the NLD child, once older, will be able to write connected words. Very little has been written about this and the answer to this question varies from child to child. From personal experience, the best thing to do is not make any changes when the child has developed a legible automatic capital handwriting.

Writing in other (scholastic) subjects

Giving an NLD child exercises that require a lot of text to be transcribed from one sheet of paper to another should be avoided. This would be too much of a burden on the child's weak level of coordination and lack of visual-spatial insight. When a dictation is being done where spelling is the most important factor, lettercards or a computer should be considered as an alternative. With tests or dictations, the NLD child must be given enough time to write the answers or lay them out with letter cards. A tape recorder can be of assistance too. An essay would be more feasible for the NLD child if it were separated into sections. Especially with long essays, a computer could be useful. When the child is graded, the teacher should base his/her judgment on quality rather than quantity.

Psychomotor coordination

The motor skills can be trained by repetitive exercises with complex movement patterns. Tying shoelaces, getting dressed, cutting, sticking, tearing, coloring without going outside the lines, holding a pencil properly, putting a key in a lock are examples of coordination that are difficult for the NLD child.

> Some of the reading and math exercises required some cutting. This was not done, as cutting would divert Joyce's attention from the ultimate aim of the exercise.

Isolated exercises of refined psychomotor coordination seem to be the best way of practicing movement patterns. These exercises need to be done between other activities and not during them. It is important to concentrate on the movement patterns involved in these actions.

> Joyce had learnt how to hold her pencil the right way by putting dots on her finger and through a pictogram of the right grip. A *gripper* or *stetro* seemed to help her in keeping three fingers on the pencil, but she put a lot of pressure on the paper. Therefore, the gripper was replaced with a slightly longer triangular piece of rubber. This triangle helped her in not pinching the pencil, but her handwriting showed signs of cramps. This seemed to be the result of the great effort Joyce had to make for the psychomotor exercise combined with the effort that she now had to make in order to spell correctly. Flapping her hands about seemed to relax her.

By way of Motor Remedial Teaching (MRT) and/or motor-sensory integration therapy, more attention can be given to motor coordination, posture and muscular tension, physical self-confidence and broadening of spatial insight. Also, relaxation techniques can help the child be more supple and make more controlled movements. In class, the child's posture when writing is most important.

> Joyce has now learnt correct posture through pictograms. They depict four steps that are required in order to be in the correct position, and are verbally explained (back straight – bottom flat – feet together – this is how I sit). By repeating the words out loud and consciously taking the

right position while saying them, Joyce mastered the posture in a few sessions. At a later stage, these pictograms were copied in a smaller format so that Joyce could keep them in her book and take them to class with her. As Joyce tends to slip into a slouching position, whenever she has a writing exercise she comes across the pictograms and adjusts her posture.

Playing with LEGO™, Duplo™ or K'NeX™, can help expand spatial-insight and increase the urge for exploration. The materials in *Modular Construction* can be used in combination with task-cards showing pictures of two- or three-dimensional constructions as an exercise. In the Netherlands, the *Cito Hulpprogramma* (Cito Help Program) has a section called *Ruimtelijk Inzicht* (Spatial Insight) that is full of great ideas for exercises with the NLD child. Games like "I see what you can't see", "Lotto", "Mazes" and "Spot the ten differences" are aimed at visual-analytic skills. Children's holiday books have many exercises of this type. To encourage the NLD child to be more aware of the "big picture", and not just interested in details, images where several things are taking place are very useful. Playing "memory" or remembering as much as possible from an image can improve the child's visual memory. The pages from the *Frostig program* offer psychomotor, spatial and visual-analytic practice.

> After a lot of practice Joyce has developed a more systematic approach in looking at and copying LEGO™ constructions. She's able to build little buildings with different colors, shapes and sizes, and remake them (referring to images from past experience). Joyce sees simple spatial structures more clearly than she used to. Her visual memory and spatial orientation seem to be in good shape. The question, however, is whether she will be able to transfer these skills to other fields.

While exploring a new space or moving around in a large space, like a gym hall, many verbal directions need to be given. Because NLD children have a hard time orientating themselves in a large space, it is necessary to give them enough time to maneuver and find their way. A clear floor plan could be useful.

Pages of work should be kept as clear and simple as possible. Enlarging the page to an A3-format, drawing a line down the middle and then drawing coloured borders around each side is useful in helping the child. Of course, an excess of colors, arrows and markings should be avoided, as they will confuse the child. All pages of exercises should be put in plastic folders in a lever arch file. This way the child can take every group of pages that go together out of the file easily, and won't be distracted by the other pages in the file. When giving the child homework, it would be wise to avoid pages full of typed text or pages that are completely handwritten (NLDline 1999b).

Socio-emotional development

Training in social skills, with the emphasis on expressing emotion and the practice of appropriate non-verbal behaviour, should also be part of the treatment of NLD. While in contact with the child, one must keep an eye on the fact that all non-verbal aspects of communication must have a verbal explanation. Just looking angry is not enough. The teacher must also say when s/he is angry. Furthermore, it is important to describe, in words, what the teacher expects from the child.

To give the NLD child a step-by-step plan or problem-solving strategy, whereby the child will be able to react to daily situations that s/he finds difficult, can give the child a lot of structure. It is worth trying to write down social rules and conventions. Group training focuses on social skills these rules and conventions, as well as giving practice in non-verbal behavior, the expression and recognition of emotions, making social contacts and expanding assertiveness. Methods like the *PAD-learning plan* (1991) or the *Box of feelings* (1999) (both Dutch publications) could lend a helping hand. An example of an exercise in recognizing people's emotions without hearing what they're saying is watching television with the sound off. Also, a collection of newspaper photos that show people's faces can help children learn about facial expressions. (NLDline 1999d). Playing with other children requires guidance from the teacher. Social frustration can be avoided by preparing the NLD child for social situations like recess or breaks. Agreeing with the child who s/he will play with and what s/he will do makes the situation clearer for the child and makes him/her feel safer. Also, there should be an option to leave the playground and go to a quieter place to calm down if necessary. The child can be helped with his/her behavior by being given an agreed-upon signal when s/he is about to burst out with anger or rage. This signal can be a short reassuring touch on the shoulder for a younger child, and for an older child, a short verbal or non-verbal signal. The difference between acceptable and unacceptable behavior must be made clear, explicitly and verbally. Good role models can be used as examples.

In social conflicts, it may be necessary to help immediately in finding a solution and *not* to get involved in a conversation with the NLD child. S/he will verbally try to get a grip on the situation, which will hinder him/her in actually doing something about it. Afterwards, the child must be encouraged to describe in detail exactly what happened, to report how the situation felt, to analyze precisely where the situation went wrong, and whose fault it was. When doing this, it is of importance that the child gets shown what is relevant or irrelevant, and to differentiate his/her vision from that of the other party. Training in "seeing it from the other person's point of view" is of the utmost importance and an important goal in the treatment of NLD children. This way, their social conscience is stimulated. For situations of social conflict that are too threatening for the NLD child, an adequate escape strategy is necessary. The child may learn to deal with his/her fears by talking about the situation (Van de Gaag, in Paternotte 2000).

Structured contact with peers may be possible if the child is sufficiently guided. However, the development of self-sufficiency is very important for the NLD child's future.

4.2 Treatment strategies at home

It is important that the parents of a child with NLD gain as much information as possible about the condition. By reading accessible articles in journals and books, or by attending parent meetings, parents will find out more about children with NLD and the complications that NLD may bring to the education of their child. From the moment parents can make the connection between their child's behavior and the neurological basis of this behavior, they can better understand their child. Home is by far the safest place to learn about compensation strategies, to teach the child basic knowledge by repetition. The home environment is both physically and emotionally trustworthy. By creating a place to play, with a mattress and a couple of cushions, the child can bounce around, fall and play without getting hurt.

Maintaining daily routine and organizing activities in small steps helps NLD children to get a clearer view of their environment. Activities can be divided up and shown on a to-do list with images and text. By laying out the child's clothes in a specific order, getting dressed can be structured and enable the child to be more independent.

Situations of transition and change demand that the parents be proactive, meaning that they should prepare things in advance and announce them. New situations are best discussed with the child beforehand and (with the help of a computer) be portrayed visually; and furthermore, the child should be accompanied by an adult in all new situations. Two aspects are most important: making order in the child's world and visualizing/describing occurrences and situations.

Parents should base their reactions more on what the child does than on what the child says. This demands that parents take an unusual position in the spectrum of parental behaviour, a fact that has been made clear by research conducted at special schools. As hard as it may be for the parent, this requires a cognitive turnaround in their approach to the child. Parents have to learn how to integrate this cognitive switch into their emotional ties with the child, and not consider it a reduction in the quality of the parent–child relationship.

Punishment of NLD children is often useless. This finding is based on the experiences of Thompson (1997b) with parents of NLD children. Parents learn to accept this when they understand that their child does not behave badly on purpose, but because of neuropsychological dysfunction. Finding the cause of the child's behavior is a more fruitful endeavor. From this viewpoint, ways of anticipating the child's behavior can be developed. Parents need to be supported in the process of learning how to deal with the behavior of their NLD child. The Home Contingency Program (HCP), a theoretical strategy for approaching problems, can be a good source of help. HCP is an empowerment program that is aimed at the restructuring and improvement of family interaction at times when things may go wrong (Miller 1975, in Dijkshoorn, Pietersen and

Dikken 1998). With this method, appropriate behavior from the NLD child is taught and rewarded.

With all of this, spontaneous fun with the child is essential and should not be forgotten.

Informing parents about the implications of the disability is important. To make sure the parents feel involved with what happens in school, they should be informed regularly about the education and adjustments that are being made on the basis of their child's needs. A so-called "back-and-forth file" (going back and forth between parents and teacher) can maintain communication. Also, the parents may want to receive information about a certain activity or issue that will be happening in school before it actually occurs. This would mean they could prepare their son or daughter for what is going to happen at school.

The approach described in this chapter does not guarantee success for every child with NLD. From personal experience, it would seem that the approach for a child with NLD constantly needs adjusting as one searches for correct methods. Because of the complexity of NLD, sudden drawbacks about something that seemed to be going well are possible. In the next section this is made clear.

4.3 Prognosis

The course of NLD has a definite effect on scholastic skills. A few remarks can be made about this. Technical reading is said to improve after a lot of repetition and practice, but reading comprehension (placing information in a new context) will still be problematic. The difference between the level of technical reading and reading comprehension just increases. Spelling eventually seems to go well, except for a few phonological errors. Mathematically, the child stays weak. After a lot of practice, at the end of primary school, the child will have developed good handwriting. In high school, the child will have a tough time as more independence and insight is required when solving new problems.

Rourke's studies (1989) show that NLD adults still have difficulty making the best of non-verbal communication and still rely very strongly on verbal information. Graauwmans (1995) speaks of a permanent handicap in processing new information. Because of problems with the brain's right hemisphere, the NLD individual will still have difficulty processing new information. NLD adults have difficulty estimating their own problems (anosognosy) and have problems finding solutions to complex situations. As a consequence, their communication with others is interrupted. Multiple and extensive guidance are part of the daily life of an adult with NLD.

As NLD individuals grow older, the interrupted development characterizes itself by shifting from externalizing problems to internalizing problems. Those with NLD have a predisposition to the development of emotional disabilities (Bigler, in Serlier-van den Bergh et al. 1997) with the possibility of isolation and exclusion. Issues around fear can be expected, as NLD individuals feel constant insecurity in relation to what may happen, how others will react and how they should behave (Thompson 1998). Those with serious mathematical problems from a technical point of view could end up being marginalized (Rourke 1993a). Fear of being in a group often occurs. Around the individual there often is not much understanding of his/her adaptive limitations. A worrying issue is that NLD individuals are at high risk of developing self-mutilating behavior, depression, fears and suicidal tendencies (Fletcher 1989, in Serlier-van den Bergh et al. 1997).

With this prognosis, the need to equip NLD children with the tools they need for the future is highlighted. NLD seems to be a structural disability that does not go away, but if the disability is discovered at an early stage, life with NLD can be rewarding.

Epilogue

This book does not cover all aspects of NLD: the descriptions within the scholastic system of the special schools highlight the problems NLD may bring in a classroom situation during remedial teaching (orthodidactic) and in what way the approach can be fine-tuned to suit the NLD child.

As far as the diagnosis research is concerned, when NLD is suspected there is no unanimity about the tests that should be taken and the interpretation of their results. In what way could young children who have not yet started school be tested? By looking at their IQ? In standardized research, how can non-verbal communication skills and socio-emotional development be tested and compared with those of children that have "normal development"? These are just a couple of questions that demand further research in order to aim diagnosis better.

Differential diagnosis is a subject area that demands a lot of attention. The way NLD relates to other learning and developmental disabilities and to what extent NLD should be in a separate category remains a point of discussion. It is of great importance to know what specific consequences working from the NLD image has for the child and the possibility of different treatments should be considered.

As to what extent NLD children can benefit from specific forms of help such as speech therapy, physiotherapy, ergotherapy, remedial teaching, sensory-motor integration therapy and play therapy, this remains an interesting question for the future. Staying informed about new publications and gathering practical insights are both necessary in the quest to find which of the above therapies can help the NLD child in his/her development and which specific adjustments and approaches are required.

The guidance of parents with an NLD child did not get emphasized in this book. The description was limited to a few focal points but these indicate the importance of maintaining contact with the parents in a scholastic environment. As there is still very little literature about specific parental support, this is definitely a subject that requires further research. Experiences from special schools, other schools and treatment institutes could possibly lead to a more directed treatment program at home. Besides giving information about, and insight into the disability, there needs to be an emphasis on actual treatment at school and at home.

It must be clear that despite the increase in people who know about NLD, there are still many uncertainties and questions. Advanced scientific research is of great importance in expanding and deepening insights surrounding NLD.

Bibliography

Achenbach, T.M (1993) *Child Behaviour Checklist / Teacher Report Form.* Dutch translation by F.C. Verhulst. Rotterdam: Academisch Ziekenhuis en Erasmus Universiteit.

Ayres, A.J. (1991) *Een behandeling voor stoornissen in de sensorische integratie. Een overzicht voor ouders, onderwijzers en andere begeleiders.* (Translation from English into Dutch was used). Santpoort-Zuid: Nederlandse Centrum voor Sensorische Integratie.

Bachot, J., Duits, P. and Graauwmans, P. (1996) "Het Syndroom van de niet-verbale leerstoornissen." *Balans Belang,* November 1996, 6–10.

Bachot, J. and Konig, C. (1999) "Behandelaspecten van kinderen met een NLD-profiel." *Congrespresentatie 10 december 1999: Het NLD-syndroom; theorie en praktijk,* 18–19. Tilbuurg/Oisterwijk: Katholieke Universiteit Braban and De Hondsberg.

Brumback, R.A., Harper, C.R. and Weinberg, W.A (2000) *Non-verbal Learning Disabilities, Asperger's Syndrome, Pervasive Developmental Disorder – Should we care ?* Internet: www.nldline.com.

Cracco, J. (1993) "Niet verbale leerproblemen: een overzicht van Rourke's model." *Tijdschrift Klinische Psychologie 23* 1, 25–46.

Cracco, J. and Thiery, E. (1993) "Neuropsychologische assessment en behandeling van een meisje met niet-verbale leerproblemen: een gevalsstudie." *Acta Ergotherapeutica Belgica 3,* 103–111.

De Kock, A.M.T. and Eilander, H.J. (1994) "Williams-Beuren-syndroom: Een aandoening van de verbindingsbanen in de hersenen ?" *Kind en Adolescent 15* 3, 133–138.

Diamond, S. (1998) Language Pragmatics and NLD. *It's As Plain As The Nose On Your Face.* Internet: www.nldonline.com.

Dijkshoorn, P., Pietersen,W and Dikken, G. (1998) *Kinderen met een contactstoornis. Een groepsbehandeling voor PDD-NOS-kinderen en hun ouders.* Lisse: Swets and Zeitlinger.

Dumont, J.J. (1994) *Leerstoornissen – deel I; Theorie en model* (pp.173–181). Rotterdam: Lemniscaat.

Eilander, H. (1992) "Neuropsychologische functiestoornissen bij aanwezigheid van een hydrocephalus." *Vriendenkring 1*, 5–12.

Foss, J.M. (1998) *Students with Non-verbal Learning Disabilities.* Internet: www.nldline.com.

Frankenberger, C. (2000) *Non-Verbal Learning Disabilities: An Emerging Profile.* Internet: www.nldline.com.

Graauwmans, P. (1995) "Niet-verbale leerstoornissen. Leer- en gedragsstoornissen vanuit een ontwikkelingsneuropsychologisch perspectief." *Signaal 11*, 25–31.

Graauwmans, P. (1997) NLD; leerstoornissen in cognitief en sociaal-emotioneel opzicht. Parallel-lezing.

Graauwmans, P. (1999) "Kenmerken van NLD bij een neuropsychologische testbatterij." *Congrespresentatie 10 december 1999: Het NLD-syndroom; theorie en praktijk,* p.17. Tilburg/Oisterwijk: Katholieke Universiteit Brabant and De Hondsberg.

Grejtak, N. (1998) "Connecting the WS (Williams Syndrome) Cognitive Profile to Educational Strategies." *WSA Newsletter* (Williams Syndrome Association). Internet: www.williams-syndrome.org/survey.htm.

Hakvoort, F.J. and Thoonen, G. (1999) "NLD en aspecten van schoolvaardigheden en -tekorten." *Congrespresentatie 10 december 1999: Het NLD-syndrooml theorie en praktijk,* 20–21. Tilburg/ Oisterwijk: Katholieke Universiteit Brabant and De Hondsberg.

Harnadek, M.C.S. and Rourke, B.P. (1994) "Principal Identifying Feature of the Syndrome of Non-verbal Learning Disabilities in Children." *Journal of Learning Disabilities. 27,* 144.

Hellemans, H. (1995) *NLD: Non-verbal Learning Diabilities. Seminarium 22 maart 1995.* Dients Kinder- en Jeugdpsychiatrie.

Hendriksen, J.G.M. (1999) "Het ontwikkelings- en neuropsychologisch profile van NLD: een beschrijving bij kinderen met neurologische ziektebeelden." *Congrespresentatie 10 december 1999: Het NLD-syndroom; theorie en praktijk,* pp.15–16. Tilburg/Oisterwijk: Katholieke Universiteit Brabant and De Hondsberg.

Jacobs, M., Sanal, G., Jackson, A. and Lewis, H. (1998) *Non-verbal Learning Disorders.* Seminar University of Georgia. Internet: www.nldline.com.

Jongepier, A.J.M. (1999a) "NLD en rekenproblemen." *Tijdschrift voor Remedial Teaching 2,* 16–20.

Jongepier, A.J.M. (1999b) "NLD en topografie." *Tijdschrift voor Remedial Teaching 3,* 30–33.

Kinsbourne, M. (1997) "Non-verbal Learning Disability." In T.E. Feinberg and M.J. Farah (eds) *Behavioural Neurology and Neuropsychology* (pp.789–794) USA: McGraw Hill Companies.

Kirk, T. (1998) *Tera's NLD Jumpstation: A Resource on non-verbal Learning Disabilities by an NLD Person.* Internet: www.geocities.com.

Klin A., Volkmar, F.R., Sparrow, S.S., Cicchetti, D.V. and Rourke, B.P.(1995) "Validity and Neuropsychological Characterization of Asperger Syndrome: Convergence with non-verbal Learning Disabilities Syndrome." *J. Child Psychology Psychiatry 36* 7, 1127–1140.

Klin A. and Volkmar, F.R. (1995) *Asperger's Syndrome: Some Guidelines for Assessment, Diagnosis and Intervention.* New Haven, Connecticut.Yale Child Study Center (Learning Disabilities Association of America).

Klin, A. Volkmar, F.R. (1996) *Asperger Syndrome: Treatment and Intervention. Some guidelines for Parents.* New Haven, Connecticut. Yale Child Study Center (Learning Disability Association of America).

Klin, A. and Volkmar, F.R. (1997) "Asperger's Syndrome." In D.J. Cohen and F.R. Volkmar (eds) *Handbook of Autism and Pervasive Developmental Disorders* (p.97–98). USA: John Wiley and Sons, Inc.

Langelaan, M. (1999) "Non-verbaal leerprobleem." *NRC Handelsblad, zaterdageditie Wetenschap en Onderwijs,* 5 Juni 1999.

Lantin,B. (1997) "Problem that is all in the mind." *Daily Telegraph* 16 September 1997.

Lieshout, E. van, Moor, J. de and Elands, E, (1999) "Rekenstoornissen bij kinderen met een neurologische beschadiging." *Congrespresentatie 10 december 1999: Het NLD-syndroom; theorie en praktijk,* p.13. Tilburg/Oisterwijk: Katholieke Universiteit Brabant and De Hondsberg.

Njiokiktijen, C.J. (1999) "Het Corpus Callosum in relatie tot het NLD-syndroom." *Congrespresentatie 10 december 1999: Het NLD-syndroom; theorie en praktijk,* pp.11–12. Tilburg/Oisterwijk: Katholieke Universiteit Brabant and De Hondsberg.

NLDline (1999a) *Education: IEP for NLD.* Internet: www.nldline.com.

NLDlin (1999b) *Helpful NLD Hints for Parents and other Caregivers.* Internet: www.nldlin.com.

NLDline(1999c) *Helpful NLD Hints for Teachers.* Internet: www.nldline.com.

NLDline (1999d) *Social Skills tips.* Internet: www.nldline.com.

Palombo, J. (1994) *Descriptive Profile of Children with NLD.* Internet: www.nldlin.com.

Paternotte, A. (1998) "Zo'n bijdehand kind. Het NLD-syndroom: oorzaken en gevolgen." *Balans Belang,* November '98, pp.3–5

Paternotte, A. (1999a) "Waarom spelt hij niet ? Het NLD-syndroom: problemen bij signalering." *Balans Belang* January 1999, pp.19–21.

Paternotte, A. (1999b) "Oren en ogen de kost geven. Het NLD-syndroom: de diagnose." *Balans Belang* March 1999, pp.18–20.

Paternotte, A. (1999c) "Leren zien door praten. Het NLD-syndroom: de behandeling." *Balans Belang* May 1999, pp.5–6.

Paternotte, A. (1999d) "Heeft Sjoerd NLD ? Zorgen om een bijzondere puber." *Balans Belang* September 1999, pp.20–22.

Paternotte, A. (1999e) "Wil 't maar niet? Trage motorische ontwikkeling bij een kind met NLD." *Balans Belang* November 1999, pp.20–22.

Paternotte,A. (2000) "Hoe denkt u over NLD? Waarom zijn kinderen met NLD zo angstig?" *Balans Belang* January 2000, pp.20–22.

Paternotte, A. and Serlier-van den Bergh, A.M.H.L. (2000) "Mogelijkerwijs NLD. Diagnose NLD nog steeds lastig." *Balans Belang*, September 2000, pp.8–10.

Richman, L. (1997) "Peaceful Coexistence – Autism, Asperger's, Hyperlexia." *American Hyperlexia Association Newsletter* Winter 1997.

Rourke, B.P. (1989) *Non-verbal Learning Disabilities. The Syndrome and the Model.* New York, London: The Guilford Press.

Rourke, B.P. (1993a) "Psychosociale dimensies van subtypen leerstoornissen: neuropsycchologische studies in het Windsor Laboratorium." *Kinderen met cerebrale ontwikkelingsstoornissen, congres de Klokkenberg – Dr. Hans Berger Kliniek*, pp. 3–7.

Rourke, B.P. (1993b) *Treatment Programme for the Child with NLD.* Canada: University of Windsor.

Rourke, B.P. (1995) *Syndrome of non-verbal learning disabilities. Neuro-developmental manifestations.* New York: Guildford Press.

Rourke, B.P. (1999a) "The non-verbal Learning Disabilities; Theory, Research and Clinical Practice." *Congrespresentatie 10 december 1999: Het NLD-syndroom, theorie en praktijk*, pp.5–7. Tilburg/Oisterwijk: Katholieke Universiteit Brabant and De Hondsberg.

Rourke, B.P. (1999b) "Niet-verbale leerstoornis. Het syndroom en het model. Verkorte bewerking." *Congrespresentatie 10 december 1999: Het NLD-syndroom; theorie en praktijk*, pp. 8–10. Tilburg/Oisterwijk: Katholieke Universiteit Brabant and De Hondsberg.

Rourke, B.P. Bakker, D.J., Fisk, J.L. and Strang, J.D. (1983) *Child Neuropsychology. An introduction to theory, research and clinical practice.* New York: The Guildford Press.

Ruijssenaars, A.J.J.M. and Ghesquiere, P. (1999) "Neuropsychologische aspecten von problematisch Leren: perspectieven en grenzen". In

A.J.J.M. Ruijssenaars and P. Ghesquiere (eds.), *Neuropsychologische aspecten van problemen op school* (pp.9–21) Leuven/Amersfoort: Acco.

Serlier-van den Bergh, A.M.H.L. (1999) "De ontwikkeling en validering van de Nederlandse NLD-schaal." *Congrespresentatie 10 december 1999: Het NLD-syndroom; theorie en praktijk*, p.14. Tilburg/Oisterwijk: Katholieke Universiteit Brabant and De Hondsberg.

Serlier-van den Bergh, A.M.H.L., Schaaijk, N. and Van der Vlugt, H. (2000) *Het gebruik van de WISC-RN bij de diagnosevorming van NLD*. Interne publicatie, in voorbereiding voor uitgave. Oisterwijk: De Hondsberg.

Serlier-van den Bergh, A.M.H.L., Smeets, C.J., Wiel, M.C.W.M van de and Vlugt, H. van der (1997) "Diagnostisering van het NLD-syndroom bij verstandelijke gehandicapte kinderen – bruikbaarheid van de experimentele non-verbale LeerStoornis-schaal." In H.M. Pijnenburg, C.M. van Rijswijk, A.J.J.M. Ruijssenaars and J.W.Veerman (eds.) *Pedologisch Jaarboek* (pp.41–56). Delft: Eburon.

Smeets, K. and Wiel, M.C.W.M. van de (1995) "Implicatien voor de schoolpraktijk bij een neuropsychologisch syndroom." *Speciaal Onderwijs 68* 9, 302–308.

Smeets, C.J. and Wiel, M.C.W.M, van de (1996) "Non-verbal Learning Disabilities. Implicaties voor behandeling bij het neuropsychologisch syndroom NLD." *Tijdschrift voor Remedial Teaching 3*, 23–26.

Thompson, S. (1996) "Non-verbal Learning Disorders." *The Gram fall/Winter Edition*. Internet: www.nldline.com.

Thompson, S. (1997a) "Non-verbal Learning Disorders revisited in 1997". *The Gram*. Internet: www.nldline.com.

Thompson, S. (1997b) *The Source for non-verbal Learning Disorders*. East Moline, Illinois: Linguisystems.

Thompson, S. (1997c) *Neurobehavioural Characteristics Seen in the Classroom – Developing an Educational Plan for the student with NLD*. Internet: www.nldline.com.

Thompson, S. (1998) *Stress, Anxiety, Panic and Phobias: Secondary to NLD*. Internet: www.nldline.com.

Vlugt, H. van der (1999) "Hydrocephalus en het NLD-syndroom." *Congrespresentatie 10 december 1999: Het NLD-syndroom; theorie en praktijk*, p.22. Tilburg/Oisterwijk: Katholieke Universiteit Brabant and De Hondsberg.

Voeller, K.K.S. (1997) "Social and Emotional Learning Disabilities." In T.E.Feinberg and M.J. Farah (eds.) *Behavioural Neurology and Neuropsychology* (pp.795–801). USA: McGraw Hill Companies.

Westrus, I. (1997) "Buitenbeentje door het NLD-syndroom?" *Sante* May 1997, pp.74–75.

Index